T0209103

Other books by Edward Schneier:

*Policy-Making in American Government* (Basic Books, 1969)

With Julius Turner, *Party and Constituency: Pressures on Congress* (Johns Hopkins University Press, 1970).

With William Murphy, *Vote Power* (Prentice-Hall, 1970; Doubleday, 1974).

*The City* (City College Press, 1983).

With Bertram Gross, *Congress Today* (St. Martin's Press, 1993).

With Bertram Gross, *Legislative Strategy* (St. Martin's Press, 1993).

With Brian Murtaugh, *New York Politics* (M. E. Sharpe, 2001 and 2009).

*The Constitution-Building Process in Indonesia* (International Institute for Democracy and Electoral Assistance, 2005).

*Crafting Constitutional Democracies* (Rowman and Littlefield, 2006).

*Muslim Democracy* (Routledge, 2016).

# Putting People Back in Politics

*The Revival of American Democracy*

Edward Schneier

authorHOUSE®

*AuthorHouse™*
*1663 Liberty Drive*
*Bloomington, IN 47403*
*www.authorhouse.com*
*Phone: 1 (800) 839-8640*

*Published by AuthorHouse 12/17/2019*

*ISBN: 978-1-7283-3936-8 (sc)*
*ISBN: 978-1-7283-3937-5 (hc)*
*ISBN: 978-1-7283-3926-9 (e)*

*Library of Congress Control Number: 2018901654*

*Print information available on the last page.*

# Contents

# Preface

This my tenth book, the first nine of which were with traditional publishing houses. I chose to self-publish this one because none of the publishers I contacted could produce a book in fewer than six months. Thanks to Authorhouse for being able to do this.

I wrote *Putting People Back in Politics* largely in response to a number of friends and neighbors who asked me– as a student of politics– what they could do to change what they see as very dangerous turns in the direction of American politics. Although the manuscript has not gone through the standard review process, I have had the very useful advice of friends and former colleagues, most of whom advised me not to be too academic. Well, old habits die hard, but I tried. And I think I have made some of the best analyses of political scientists and professionals accessible if not always exciting. You can skip through some of the material if you like, but if you truly want to work for change I think it will be worth your while to read on. Many of the most sincere and dedicated activists I know are, unfortunately, wasting their time or actually acting in ways that might even be counter-productive. Politics remains as much art as science. It is, at the same time, a well-studied activity that operates according to increasingly well-understood rules. While there are no clear rules of political efficacy, there are ways of doing things that are manifestly more effective than others.

I want particularly to thank Ellen Boneparth, Ron Hayduk, Virginia Martin, Gareth Rhodes, Ken Sherrill, Christina Russenello, Elliot Schneier, Jeff Stonecash, Lynda Stratigos and above all my wife Margrit for their help and comments.

# Introduction

# Putting People Back in Politics

Seldom in American politics has there been an eruption of political activism comparable to that which arose in the wake of the 2016 elections. Literally tens of millions took to the streets and town meetings offering time, money and passion to the causes of peace, good government, civil rights and economic justice. Most of them were wasting their time. In politics, sincerity and conviction win grace points but little influence. Even money– the "mother's milk of politics"– doesn't make much of a difference if it is poorly spent; and the sad fact is that much of it is.

On the other side, hundreds of thousands of people– many of them mobilized and connected by and through these town halls and demonstrations– took to the streets in another manner to begin the process of actually changing the system. In 2018, a record number of citizens reported having worked in a political campaign. Many of them were effective.

The purpose of this book is to offer a short guide to effective political action, particularly in the realms of political campaigns and legislative advocacy. The premise, that ordinary people can make a difference, has become almost quaint. Political campaigns and political advocacy (also known as lobbying) have been professionalized to the point where citizens are treated more as audiences than participants. This is not to denigrate the skills of political professionals, most of whom are very good at what they do. In becoming more effective citizens we can learn a lot from those for whom politics is a way to make a living. But in making a case that ordinary people can make a difference, I also want to argue that they should. As smart and capable as most political consultants and lobbyists are, they have become the core actors in an increasingly dysfunctional system. Real change can come only when we put people back in politics. Putting people back in politics is not just effective as a strategy, it is good for democracy. More than ever we need to revive and extend a culture of participation that involves treating us as citizens rather than consumers. What follows here is not simply a "how to" manual, but a "why to" screed on the state of our polity and what needs to be done to bring the country back from a slide toward authoritarianism, intolerance and dysfunction.

There are all kinds of ways in which elections are won and lost. Sophisticated uses of polls, social media, computer algorithms and advertising are claimed to be able increasingly to target and deliver blocs of voters to those candidates who can afford them. Campaign management has become a big business. Between elections, similarly sophisticated paid lobbyists exert a strong influence on behalf of those who can best afford to hire them. The premise here, however, is that in the long run nothing is more effective than a well-organized movement of average citizens. Clever advertising can swing votes, but nothing is more effective than direct contact with someone you already know. Facts and numbers count for a lot in lobbying, as does money, but nothing is more effective than testimony from an informed constituent as to how the law impacts real people in a legislator's district.

In 1970 my then co-author, William T. Murphy, Jr. and I wrote a book called *Vote Power* as handbook for student volunteers working under the umbrella of the Princeton-based Movement for a New Congress which helped elect a number of anti-war Representatives and Senators in the midterm elections. While the Movement was successful in channeling the energies of activists into electoral politics, it was neither intended nor able to follow up its election victories with policy advocacy. The war dragged on for another four years, and while many of the Senators and House members it helped elect became effective spokespersons for progressive causes, the students who helped elect them, in effect, went back to their classrooms.

Murphy and I published a second edition of the book in 1974 when Nixon's Watergate problems were closing in, and the failure of our intervention in Vietnam was widely perceived. As we moved through the 1970s, however, the allure of citizen participation in politics was fading. A whole new cadre of political campaign professionals took over the management of most state, local and national election campaigns. They replaced the rusty, often moribund party organizations and political machines that had been at core of political campaigns for nearly a century. While few mourned the passing of the Daley organization in Chicago or New York's Tammany Hall, the rise of what became known as "candidate-centered campaigns" has taken us into a not-so-brave new world of political dysfunction. The premises of *Vote Power,* with its emphasis on face-to-face politics was becoming quaint.

"In the wake of Watergate," Murphy and I wrote in 1974, "political cynicism is reaching an all-time high. No lecture on democratic theory is going to convince many Americans that corruption is not part and parcel of the electoral process."[1] Forty plus years later, these perceptions have, if anything, become increasingly more negative. Consider the state of our major political institutions. In a 2016 Gallup survey of citizen trust in their political institutions, the Supreme Court and the Presidency were rated "very" or "somewhat" worthy of trust by just 36%; the Congress by just 9%. The last time a majority of Americans trusted the Court was in 2002; the Presidency in 2009; and not once since the 1970s has Congress earned majority support.[2] Academic studies provide little encouragement. In 2006, Thomas E. Mann, of the generally liberal Brookings Institution, and Norman J. Ornstein of the conservative American Enterprise Institute titled their study of Congress "The Broken Branch: How Congress is Failing America and How to Get It Back on Track." The title of the follow-up study, published in 2012, "It's Even Worse than It Looks: How the American Constitutional System Collided With the New Politics of Extremism," pretty much sums up the consensus of how political scientists view recent developments.[3]

Cynicism, doubt and despair, no matter how warranted, are wasted emotions unless backed with incentives to act. And the only kinds of effective acts available to most of us involve working within the institutional structures already in place. We don't need Syria to remind us that armed resistance is fruitless in a garrison state, a "cure" probably worse than the disease. Demonstrations are useful tools of consensus building, publicity and mobilization, but they change nothing. Tea Party demonstrations in 2014 and 2015 did help to create networks of believers, their bonds strengthened by social media that began to bear fruit only when they were linked to political campaigns and backed by the financial and professional resources of very traditional Republican Party and wealthy interest groups. For those seeking change not catharsis, there are really only two kinds of effective political action. In the words of the Princeton's Institute of Advanced Study political theorist Michael Walzer,

> The two kinds are pressure politics and electoral politics, and I am inclined to think there are no other kinds. To choose pressure politics means to try to influence those people who already hold power, who sit in official seats, and who may even be responsible for the outrages against which the movement is aimed. To choose electoral politics is to try to dislodge those people and to plant others in their seats. . . . Of course, the two choices overlap in important ways . . . but it is worth emphasizing the two simply because they exhaust the range: changing the policies men [and women] make and changing the men [and women] who make policies. Changing the political system within which policy is made is rarely a real option for citizen activists.[4]

To put a more positive spin on Dr. Walzer's last point, changing the system in which policy is made *is* possible, but only, ironically, by changing or influencing the people who are already in office. *To change the rules of the game, in other words, one must first change the rule-makers.* Whatever the social goals which motivate people to involve themselves in politics, the best way to achieve those goals is to elect candidates who share them or to scare the hell out of those who do not. Some politicians are shrewd. Some are simply dumb. Some are corrupt and can be bought. All know how to count votes. Nothing is more important to the future of American society than the way in which those votes are distributed. On election night they don't count issues, preferences or emotions; they count votes. And between elections, politicians don't look back, they think about the next election.

Professionals have important roles to play in campaigns: election laws, particularly those regarding campaign finance are complex and important. Professionals are, by definition, less likely to accept the often-biased assurances of local "leaders" who will say things like "don't worry about the third ward, I've got that covered," or "don't even bother with Mudville, they're all against us." Even in small-town local elections, it is useful to have someone other than the candidate to take the heat for some necessary decisions (like telling the local nutcake why his or her help is not wanted, or explaining why the candidate cannot be in two places at the same time). There is, moreover, a whole library of books, and a large industry of trained and experienced campaign managers who understand how to conduct and use public opinion polls, create effective promotional materials, make media buys, and so on. Even the best managed of these campaigns, however, leave something to be desired, and a strong case can be made the very paradigm on which the professional campaign edifice is built has become increasingly less effective.

Concerned citizens can make a difference, especially when they understand the changes in our political system that have increasingly divorced public policy from public attitudes. The old British adage that trained civil servants should be kept on tap but not on tap applies with special force to professional political operatives. For although there are things that require expert knowledge– every campaign, for example, needs access to legal advice, media buys, voter targeting, financial reporting and fund raising– too many modern campaigns are run by very talented people with all these skills but little knowledge of the districts in which they are working. In 2016, there were many active Democrats in Ohio, Pennsylvania and Wisconsin who could have told Hilary Clinton that her campaign was floundering; her very smart campaign professionals didn't figure that out until election night.

Let us at the outset be very clear about the very real limits of citizen power. Any individual's personal influence is likely to be small. Your vote, in any given election, is unlikely to affect the outcome: in a typical congressional district in 2018 it was as little as $1/350,000^{th}$ of the total. Many, if not most legislative districts, moreover, have been constructed as to not be competitive. Running against incumbents has always been especially difficult. In 2016, 97% of the members of the House and 93% of Senators running for re-election won, and they were only marginally less successful in 2018 when the re-election rates were 91.2% in the House and 83% in the Senate.

To those political convictions are strong perhaps the most frustrating aspect of political activity comes from dealing with their fellow citizens who don't know, don't care and don't vote. The fight among activist thus turns frequently on who can turn out the faithful. And this is not easy. Non-voters are non-voters for a reason, sometimes out of active hostility to all things political, more frequently out a deep-seated apathy difficult for politically active people to understand.

Equally frustrating for many activists is the discovery that issue voting– at least in the way democratic theory describes it– is rare. To the true believer, finding someone who agrees with them on most issues but is voting for the opposing candidate because she seems honest, has run a successful business, hasn't had an affair, or who looks like a congressman, can be very frustrating. And then there are the single issue people, found among both voters and volunteers. In most campaigns, you really are selling "lesser-evilism," a pragmatic calculus– all things considered– that voting for one candidate or another will in the long run, considering all issues, make the country a better place. When it works, ours is a representative democracy in which we elect people not to put all of our desires into policy, but to work with others in at least partially satisfying as many as possible. Unless you are looking in a mirror, you will seldom see a perfect candidate, nor will that perfect candidate be able to see all of his or her preferences enacted into law. Vanity voters, who see voting as an expressive rather than instrumental act, can be as frustrating as hard core opponents.

The extreme form of vanity voting is support for third parties. The math is very simple. Let us suppose that you are a Democrat who believes that the "powers that be" in the party keep coming up with candidates who are "too centrist," "too beholden to Wall Street," or whatever, and you are convinced that a third party candidate could win at least a third of the vote. OK, here's the math. Take that third of the total vote (say 33,333 of 100,000 votes in the general election; the "Wall Street Democrat" wins 25,000. Thus the two Democrats between them win 58,333; but they lose to a Freedom caucus Republican who gets fewer than 42,000. Instead of a lesser evil Democrat, both the leftists and the centrists wind up being represented by someone they both agree is truly evil. Run that same candidate in the Democratic primary and your 33,000 votes win the nomination in a walk and almost certainly go on to victory in November.

What most third party advocates and many partisans do not recognize is just how vulnerable the major parties are. While they differ between the parties and among the states, the essential building blocs start at the level of local election districts or precincts where enrolled party members "run" in primaries. Typically, these races are almost never competitive: anyone who can get the ten or twenty signatures to get the nomination will be able to run unopposed. My son and daughter-in-law, typically, live in semi-rural district in New Jersey where six of the eight district committee seats were vacant. Essentially all it takes to become a part of the party "power structure" is to raise your hand. It gets more difficult and complicated as one moves up to the county or ward or assembly district level, then to the state and national committees, but the process at all levels– and in both major parties– is wide open. The real powers of these organizations– especially vis a vis incumbent office holders– vary; but they are almost always far more permeable than most outsiders think.

This is not a campaign manual. It doesn't instruct potential candidates how to run, nor how one gets a voter file from the Board of Elections. It has no canned scripts for volunteers. There are plenty of good books that do that. What it does try to do is to make sense of a political system that is not working very well, and to try to provide some glimmers of hope, and some concrete steps to be taken by those who believe in democratic change. Beyond election-related activities, it is also a roadmap of sorts to political influence between elections. This is not a book for everyone. It is aimed, quite specifically, at those who are frightened, frustrated and flummoxed by Donald Trump's election and that of the members of Congress who have worked with him radically to redirect our politics. It is aimed at those who deplore the development of "alternative facts," the rejection of science and "the toxic confluence of arrogance, narcissism and cynicism that Americans now wear like a full suit of armor against experts and professionals."[5] And it is for people who oppose rather than welcome the growing openness and acceptance of racial and ethnic political prejudice. Conservatives may find some of its practical suggestions useful, but will probably find its liberal bias too tendentious to ignore. And that's fine. The smoothest road to the restoration of "small d" democracy, I am convinced, runs now through the Democratic Party, and it that sense what follows has a "big D" Democratic tilt. The hope for political reform, however, is not partisan and nothing would be more pleasing than have Republican partisans take its message to heart as well.

# Endnotes

1   William T. Murphy, Jr. and Edward Schneier, Vote Power: How to Work for the Person You Want Elected (Garden City, NY: Anchor Books, 1974), viii.

2   Http://www.Gallup.com/poll/1597/confidence-institutions.aspx. Accessed, April 25, 2017.

3   Thomas E. Mann and Norman J. Ornstein, The Broken Branch: How Congress Is Failing America and How to Get it Back on Track (New York: Oxford University Press, 2006) and Mann and Ornstein, It's Even Worse than It Looks: How the American Constitutional System Collided With the New Politics of Extremism (New York: Oxford, 2012).

4   Michael Walzer, Political Action: A Practical Guide to Movement Politics (Chicago: Quadrangle Books, 1971), pp. 25-26.

5   Tom Nichols, The Death of Expertise: The Campaign Against Established Knowledge and Why It Matters (New York: Oxford University Press, 2017), 3.

# Chapter 1

# The Changing Face of American Politics

*Executive Summary and Action Plan*

Our system of government is failing. As the country falls deeper into an abyss of polarization, dysfunction and mistrust, the very people who could and should do most to change it are increasingly alienated from politics. At the same time, the American political system is far more open to activists than most of them believe. Getting involved in politics is important not just in the short run, but in the larger sense of putting our democratic system back together.

The starting point for change, and the most viable pathway to reform is through electoral politics. And because it is both more vulnerable and receptive to reform, the most accessible vehicle is the Democratic Party. This chapter explains how the demise of the Democrats has combined with the professionalization of politics increasingly to isolate office-holders from their constituents. Although the Party's decline is rooted partially in demographic patterns and discriminatory election laws, many of the Party's problems are of its own making. Its fundamental economic and social justice orientations have been distorted less by substantive policies than through top-down, money-driven methods of running for office. Although its campaign professionals have developed increasingly sophisticated methods of delivering votes, the bloodless, impersonal nature of these techniques has robbed the party of authenticity.

1

The first step in putting people back in politics is to revive or replace party organizations that have become empty shells. It is vital to grasp the importance of capturing the nominating process, the most crucial but least understood aspect of politics. In most parts of the country, party nominations can be won organizations taken over with fractions of the popular vote. Effective activism begins with an understanding of how this process works.

The 2018 elections provided an opportunity to begin the process of changing the increasingly dysfunctional Congress. While sometimes abrasive and poorly prepared, a dozen or so very different kinds of Democrats were elected in 2018, many through the kinds of grassroots campaigns championed in this book. And they are already having an impact. Both parties need more legislators with ties to their districts strong enough to counter the centralizing forces of party discipline and big money. The next steps toward reform begin with those more actively involving citizens in politics.

## The Importance of Participation

One of the few things on which supporters of the Tea Party, Bernie Sanders and Alexandria Ocasio-Cortez agree is that the American political system is functioning badly. As party polarization intensifies, our sense of a civic culture and its related values of comity, courtesy and compromise have evaporated into a toxic atmosphere of alienation and mistrust. As with most swings in national mood, recent manifestations of dysfunction are most vividly on display in Congress which— to give it its due— has rather faithfully recorded and amplified much of what is wrong with our politics. There is a vicious circle here: "deepening public disillusionment . . . has been both cause and effect of policy paralysis"[1]

The waves of discontent that have roiled American waters have washed over other shores as well, bringing dark undercurrents of authoritarianism and intolerance. After years of touting the spread of democracy, the respected *Journal of Democracy* increasingly features gloomy tales of rising authoritarianism. "Even in some of the richest and most politically stable regions of the world," as one recent essay put it, "it seems as if democracy is in a serious state of disrepair."[2] In both the United States and Europe there is a growing tendency for younger people in particular to describe "having a democratic political system" as a "bad" or "very bad" way to "run the country."[3] An infectious, often prejudiced form of nationalistic xenophobia has re-emerged as a significant political force even in countries long thought to have put that sad story behind them. In most of the world's putative democracies, moreover, recent decades have seen a slow but continuous decline in both citizen participation and trust in political institutions.

Democratic governance is strongly correlated with participatory cultures: educational systems that encourage dialogue over rote learning, neighborhood associations that actually meet, businesses in which employers and employees work together, and even social organizations where people learn the skills of interaction. From Alexis de Tocqueville's 1835 *Democracy in America* to Robert Putnam's *Bowling Alone,* the link between a vigorous associational life and democracy has long been clear. Civic groups produce "virtuous circles" of trust and habits of accommodation, serving as what Tocqueville called "large free schools" in democracy. Bowling alone, as opposed to bowling in a league, provides no such experience.[4] It is through working with others that people become citizens rather than subjects. The less people participate in governance, conversely, the less they believe they can.

Putting people back in politics can have the salutary effects both of making people feel better about the way the system works, and of making those in government more accessible. The better one knows people in power– whether in business, education or government– and the better they know their employees and constituents, the more they become "just folks." Years ago, I asked my one-time boss, former Senator Birch Bayh, what made him think he could run for President. "The better I got to know the other candidates," he said, "the more I felt that I was as well-qualified as them." Too often, today's politicians– like the retired congressman who ruefully confessed that he had forgotten how to use his own umbrella– have ceased to see themselves or be seen by others as real people. Those in government– the "establishment" if you will– too often lose touch with ordinary people. In campaigns they rely increasingly on raising enough money to hire sophisticated campaign professionals who run media-focused campaigns. Add to that the personal isolation and the barriers of staff and media that separate politicians from daily contacts with ordinary people, and the system is in trouble.

Clearly some people have a lot more power and influence than others. Conspiracies, cabals, networks of corruption do exist. But it is more the complexity of power than its concentration that makes the system dysfunctional and difficult to change. The greater the power distance between citizens and their government, the less likely either is to work well. The first step on the road to closing this gap is to understand the system's complexity and the key points of access to it. The road to change in 2020 is through electoral politics and the most available vehicle to travel it is the Democratic Party.

## The Demise of the Democrats

Democrats have had at least a slight advantage in the percentage of people identifying with a party almost every year since Gallup began surveying party preferences in 1991. Before the 2018 elections, Republicans controlled the White House, the House of Representatives, the Senate, 32 of 50 Governorships and 67 of 98 partisan state legislative houses. Their margin of seats in state legislatures was 4100 to 3200, despite the edge Democrats still enjoyed in expressed voter support. Clearly the Democrats are being outplayed. And despite their 2018 successes in races for the House and state legislatures they lost ground in the Senate, remain about 600 state legislative seats behind (a net margin of 47% to 53%), and are ahead by only 54% to 46% in the House.

In part, the Democrats misfortunes are rooted in demographics. Urban areas and areas of high poverty remain at the core of the party's voting constituency. These voters are concentrated to the extent that they form what amounts to a natural gerrymander or what academics call partisan clustering. Gerrymandering works by maximizing seats in the legislature by winning a lot of districts by small margins and losing a few by landslides. In a similar matter, partisan clustering, in which Democrats are concentrated in urban districts where they win by large margins, in effect "wastes" Democratic votes. In the 2016 elections for the State Senate in New York, to use a somewhat extreme example, 22 of the 31 Democrats who won (20 of them in New York City) did so with 90% of the vote or more. Only 6 of 30 Republicans won by similarly lopsided margins, or, to put it another way, it took the Republicans fewer votes to win more seats. Even in the Democrat's landslide victory in 2018, it took 64% of the popular vote to win 62% of the seats. Although there is a gerrymandering factor that explained the Republican's previous ability to maintain control of the State Senate, partisan clustering was and is a key factor.[5] Democratic voters are packed into urban areas less by gerrymandering than by patterns of residency founded in economics, ethnicity, race and choice. Nationally, a similar combination of gerrymandering and demographics has produced a House of Representatives in which "very few representatives (twenty-nine to be precise) now serve in districts without a clear partisan tilt."[6] The Electoral College similarly disadvantages Democrats in the Presidential vote.

Economic segregation has also impacts the Democratic vote by creating a "class gap" in participation. Poorer neighborhoods, with fewer competitive elections and less vibrant civic cultures, lack the time, political resources and skills more readily available to the affluent. This gap "helps perpetuate a virtuous cycle of engagement and responsiveness among the prosperous and a vicious cycle of isolation and disengagement among the impoverished."[5] And this has helped create a parallel problem for the Party. "The economic segregation of wealth has made it easier and less costly to target neighborhoods with stronger civic environments– specifically, robust social networks, active voluntary associations and higher levels of education and income."[6] Add to this increasingly expensive campaigns that rely on affluent donors, and the Democrats, as a party, find themselves increasingly distanced from their base. Republicans, meanwhile, have been increasingly aggressive in using their new majorities to aggravate this gap by revising the rules of the game. Adding deliberate gerrymanders to demographic disparities they have virtually locked in their legislative majorities. Further tipping the balance, they have enacted state-level election rules specifically aimed at disenfranchising the poor, particularly those in urban areas.[7]

The cumulative effects of these factors are striking. In most elections since the Supreme Court ruled that districts must be of roughly equal size, the party winning the most popular votes usually won a bonus of a few seats in the House. In 1996, however, the Democrats won a majority of the total popular vote, but only 47.6% of House seats. Only twice since then (in 2008 and 2018) have Democrats won a higher percentage of seats than votes, and the differential is growing. In 2014, Republicans won 56.8% of the seats with only 53% of the vote. In 2016, the Democrats total of 48.9% of the major party congressional vote gained them only 44.6% of the seats– the biggest discrepancy between seats and votes (4.3%) in modern history.[8] These trends were slightly reversed in 2018 when the Democrats won a record 53.4% of the popular vote and 54.1% of the seats; but even here Republicans were able to hold onto 199 seats despite a record low 44.8% of the popular vote.

As much as these factors help explain the Democrats under-performance in recent elections, many of the larger problems are of their own making. Since the election of Donald Trump, Democrats have been arguing about the message the party should be sending to voters. To critics of the Party's "establishment," its leadership has been too close to Wall Street and too far from tapping into the aspirations of its base voters. If the Democrats moved left, it is argued, if they more vigorously espoused policies that redistribute income, they could have won major victories in 2016. "If only" questions are always problematic in politics; but his one, despite its apparent simplicity, is particularly opaque.

To begin with, voters had no problem distinguishing Clinton and Trump on economic issues, and by margins that make it difficult unlikely that a change in either candidates' positions on economic issues could substantially have changed the outcome.[9] The dominant narrative of the campaign– that the Democrats lost because they failed to reach working class and lower income voters with a more progressive platform– is, at best, weakly supported. Polls taken during the campaign rather consistently showed issues of "character" and recondite but apparently significant "issues" such as Benghazi and Clinton's e-mails often exceeding economic concerns in the eyes of voters, particularly among those with lower education. Lurking in the background, though difficult to survey, were issues of race and ethnicity. When Clinton moved left to adopt positions similar to those of Bernie Sanders on college tuition, the effects on public opinion were negligible. Congressional candidates who ran to the left of Clinton, moreover, did not run particularly well. Clinton lost Wisconsin, for example, by a margin of just 23,000 votes; but the progressive Russ Feingold lost his Senate race by 99,000. Ted Strickland, similarly lost his Ohio race by 11.4% compared with Clinton's 8.6.

If economic issues had few direct effects in 2016, perceptions did. And it could well be that it was less Clinton's actual stands than perceptions of her "real" loyalties and positions that hurt most. Robert Reich put it as follows:

> The Democratic Party as it is now constituted has become a giant fundraising machine, too often reflecting the goals and values of the moneyed interests. This must change. . . .The election of 2016 has repudiated it. We need a people's party — a party capable of organizing and mobilizing Americans in opposition to Donald Trump's Republican Party... What happened in America Tuesday should not be seen as a victory for hatefulness over decency. It is more accurately understood as a repudiation of the American power structure.[10]

This brings us a lot closer to understanding why Clinton, and Democrats more generally, failed in 2016. The Democrat's message can be tinkered with for sure; but the road to change is less through complex policy arguments than through a major shake-up in its top-down, elitist, money-driven methods of running for office. When the campaign and its priorities are all there is, the medium, to recycle Marshall McLuhan's aphorism, has become the message. The modern campaign, whether at the national, state or local level; whether Republican or Democratic, has become more an expensive technology-intensive bureaucratic battle of campaign professionals than a contest between politicians, partisans and political activists. With few exceptions, all campaigns have come to look pretty much alike.

## The Professionalization of Politics

In the 1950s and 60s, spurred by the emergence of television as a cultural influence, a new kind of politics emerged in the United States. Party organizations were increasingly replaced by candidate-centered coalitions run by increasingly specialized cadres of campaign professionals. The hierarchy of party leaders, from precinct captains to ward leaders to state chairs was displaced by "nearly 75 different categories of campaign professionals, including crisis management, grassroots strategy, digital mapping, media and speech training, online information services, referendum consulting, and more."[11] Gone was good-old-Charlie who knew everyone in the Fifth Ward. Instead there were experts in data analytics, many of whom had no real knowledge or particular interest in politics and public policy.

The modern campaign begins with money. One professional campaign consultant told me recently that he wouldn't work for a congressional candidate who hadn't already raised at least $200,000. The next step, as a rule, is to hire professionals and design a strategy for reaching potential supporters. For many years, this was done almost entirely through survey research. Candidate polls– unlike the horse race-who's ahead polls you find in the media– are directed less at questions of who is winning than on how various demographic groups are likely to respond to particular kinds of appeals. In the media age, voters became less individual targets than larger networks of potential supporters matched according to polling data, demographics and media usage. Thus, for example, if the survey finds that senior citizens are worried about Medicare, you produce commercials on that issue for media outlets with older audiences. Although this kind of targeting was relatively crude, it was reasonably effective,[12] and most candidates for major office continue to use such polls.

Polling, however, has significant (and growing) limitations. In just over a decade, the percentage of households using cell phones as opposed to land lines has gone from near zero to nearly sixty percent, making it more difficult to match respondents to their physical addresses. What are much harder to overcome are the biases that come from systems that identify or block calls, and from the growing number of people who refuse to be surveyed. One source of error in the 2016 surveys in some states, for example, was the failure of some pollsters to take into consideration different response rates associated with education.[13] It is possible to correct such errors by (the expensive way) polling more people or statistically "adjusting" the results by giving added weight to less educated respondents; but the more you do this, the less "random" your sample and the less reliable the results.

It gets worse. In the campaign poll, as opposed to one simply measuring who's ahead, it is the subcategories that are of prime concern. With gender dividing half male and half female, a sample of 1200 now becomes 600 which still yields an acceptable margin of error; but if you want to check, say urban, suburban and rural women, or low, high and medium income males, the cell sizes shrink to the point where the margins of error can go up to double digits. And if you to pull out, say Latino, middle income males you may be making inferences from the responses of as few as ten people, not a reliable sample at all.

One final problem with polls is in deciding what to ask and how to code the answers. The more nuanced the issue question, the more you risk not completing the survey and confusing less educated respondents. On a complicated issue like health care, for example, the question of whether one supports repealing and replacing "Obamacare" will get a different response from one inquiring about the "Affordable Care Act," and either question might misleadingly get affirmative answers from those who support (a) eliminating any government role and (b) enlarging it into a single-payer system. The kinds of broad numbers generated by polls were good enough in the age of mass media when a relatively small number of media outlets reached a large proportion of the population; but as these outlets become more segmented, the need for more specialized data grows.

Cable television, streaming and other media continue rapidly to fragment audiences. Even on traditional networks, audiences are becoming increasingly less concentrated. For roughly seventy years, the A.J. Nielsen Company has tracked the audiences for television showings, rating each program's share of viewers. Here are Nielsen's top-rated shows for each of the last seven decades:

1951-60 (I Love Lucy): 67.3
1961-70 (Beverly Hillbillies): 39.1
1971-80 (All in the Family): 34.0
1981-90 (The Cosby Show): 34.9
1991-2000 (E. R.): 22.0
2001-2010 (American Idol): 17.6
2011-18 (NCIS): 13.5

In the years since 2011, in other words, nearly ninety percent of those watching television at any given time were watching something other than the top-rated show. And there are fast growing numbers– among younger people especially– who do not watch broadcast television at all.

This fragmentation of the media dramatically changes the need for data. Just as sample surveys lose reliability as they try to segment the population into subcategories of gender, ethnicity, education, and so on, they simply cannot monitor audience preferences for such diverse media menus. Whether out of simple habit or the inability to develop more sophisticated models, most campaigns continue to act, in part at least, as if nothing had really changed. Painting with a broad brush, one campaign looks pretty much like another. The Wesleyan Media project in fact found that 69% of all Democratic ads in 2018 were about health and Medicare; 66% of Republican ads about taxes or health.

Increasingly, however, though almost as if in a parallel universe, new models of voter targeting are surging in importance. Thus the development of complex data banks and algorithms that combine poll data, canvassing results, computer site selections, demographics and campaign donation records, and even such things as membership in the Audubon Society to identify communities of identity, interest, emotion, affinity and peer networks that can be used to identify, target, package and deliver voters.[14] These high technology techniques have revolutionized electoral politics to the point at which the "post-modern" candidate is more a piece "in a complex communication environment, rather than driving these developments."[15] Extend this argument only slightly, and it suggests that we are moving to a system in which it is the campaigns rather than the candidates that are the driving force. Thus, in many ways, the campaign industry has increasingly morphed into a war of targeting, of making custom lists of who to contact how. From a mass media approach, where the goal was to maximize exposure to large groups of voters, the "post-modern" campaign seeks to develop "a carefully honed message directed to each persuadable voter group. Contemporary electioneering uses a rifle, not a shotgun. It is the art and science of modern campaign 'targeting.'"[16]

As campaigns have changed, so have those who run for office. Once there was a more or less regular progression up the political ladder from party work to local and state offices and on to Congress or the state legislature. In recent sessions of Congress, for the first time in modern history, fewer than half of the members of the House and Senate had served previously in state legislatures.[17] More lateral entry, by-passing party organizations in favor of candidates with money and celebrity appeal has shifted the ground from debates and press reports to campaign controlled paid media. In the extreme case, candidates seldom appear anywhere but at their own tightly scripted events.

Modern campaign technologies are often criticized for packaging candidates as if they were toothpaste or soap. In fact what professional campaigns package are voters. The post-modern campaign both replicates and improves upon the ward politics of old by, in effect, changing the concept of the ward from that of a geographic unit to a social network constituted through technology. "While the 'wards' of the past were defined geographically and at times as legal units of political representation, today they are expansive spaces of mediated social relations that encompass the geographic communities, families, professional and identity affiliations, and acquaintances of supporters."[18] The interactions between and among these networks, at the same time, are not the kinds of unmediated communications that take place face to face. They are essentially bloodless, more in the nature of semi-connected monologues than human conversations. Most campaigns, as Hersh puts it, focus "not on real *voters* per se, but rather on *perceived voters*. . . . They are not people; they are avatars generated from whatever data a political campaign, candidate, or party can surmise."[19]

Thus although there is little doubt that technology can dramatically expand the scope of political communications and the size of the community, it is not at all clear that there is any real dialogue taking place. Theda Skocpol, Harvard Professor of Government and Sociology, puts this in personal terms:

> Every month or so, I get a letter from some Democratic Party office: a long, canned statement, hopelessly bland, accompanied by a fake questionnaire, a tear-out wallet "membership card," and– of course, the real point– a return card and envelope for me to use to send a big check. The party tells me, in the form letter, that it wants my opinions. But it really just wants my money so it can pay pollsters and consultants. In turn, party officials, or consultants hired by the party, tell individual candidates how to word their media messages and speeches. . . The consultants pretty much are the Democratic Party. In most communities and states, there are few opportunities for regular Democrats to talk with one another, or to talk back to the consultants

and candidates. The people who talk to one another are the consultants.[20]

It need not work this way. The new technologies can be used in ways that supplement and strengthen rather than displace volunteers on the ground. With help from the data bases, volunteers can have "more information at their fingertips than they would have with conventional walk lists, including basic information on members of their neighbors' households (e.g., ages, party affiliation, registration status, and the results of prior canvasses)."[21] At the same time, continuing tensions between number crunchers and amateurs and between national organizations and local forces are inevitable, as are, what one of Obama's key advisors described as a tension between "the desire to be authentic and the desire to be super-duper effective."[22]

## Learning from Tammany Hall

The old machines died for a number of reasons. A better educated electorate increasingly rejected their paternalistic culture. The welfare state made their direct help to the needy less necessary. As incomes rose, their patronage jobs became less attractive. And their own excesses increasingly made them targets of ridicule and scorn. In a larger sense, however, the interpersonal, face-to-face politics of the old organizations lost its relevance to a more mobile, media-oriented politics. With polling and carefully crafted commercials the modern campaign was able to go over the heads of the old precinct captains and reach mass audiences through television. The post-modern campaign holds the promise returning campaigns to the grassroots, working, ironically, through the formal organizational structures of the major parties that remain essentially unchanged. The basic building block of the organization was and still is the precinct (sometimes known as an election district), usually composed of roughly a thousand registered voters, whose party members elect two captains. These precinct captains typically meet at least once a year to elect the next level of officers, which are called county committee members in some areas, ward leaders in many urban areas, or district leaders (covering, for example, the districts used to elect members of the state assembly). They in turn elect the members of the state committees of each party, who in turn elect representatives to the national committees. In their day, strong party organizations like New York's Tammany Hall, the Daley organization in Chicago, the Republican organizations on New York's Long Island, and the Cox machine in Cincinnati, Ohio decided who would run as the party's candidates; who would get jobs in city, county and, sometimes, state offices; and, frequently, who would win government contracts. Often corrupt, these party machines nonetheless played an important role, particularly in the early 1900s in bringing immigrants into the system; bringing order to fragmented, ineffective governments; and "providing avenues of social mobility for the otherwise disadvantaged."[23] There are virtually no effective political machines, Republican or Democratic, in the United States today; but there are still lessons to be learned from both their successes and failures and in comparison with the campaign systems that displaced them.

The problem of the typical machine politician was his or her inability to move past organizational norms more oriented toward favor trading and patronage than good public policy. The machine, however, knew that its survival depended on its ability to nominate candidates who were both loyal and (more importantly) electable. The problem with today's self-recruited candidate is that he or she might not be either.

*The beginning point of wisdom for citizen activists is the importance of recapturing the nominating process.*

Many years ago, one of the sharpest of the old machine's practitioners, Frank Kent, pointed out that if the organization "loses in the primaries, it is out of business."[24] So it remains today with anyone seeking political power. In all but a handful of states, "candidates of the two great parties must first be nominated as a result of primaries."[25] It is a continuing source of wonder how few Americans understand this basic fact. By refusing to register with a party in the sixteen states with closed primaries almost a third of American voters have given up their right to participate in this process.[26] Of those allowed to vote in primaries, moreover, it is striking how few do. Here is a case from my co-authored text on New York politics that is extreme but illustrative. It involves Patrick Manning, a member of the New York State Assembly, who for years had run unopposed in either the primary or general election.

When Manning embarked on a brief campaign for governor in 2006, a local mayor decided to challenge him in the Republican primary for his assembly seat. Fewer than 6,000 voters turned out in the September primary, giving the upstart, Marcus Molinaro of Tivoli, the Republican line by a margin of just 2,770 to 2,539. Molinaro's opponent in the November general election was an unusually vigorous and articulate candidate, but despite lingering divisions in the Republican Party, she lost to Molinaro by a margin of 22,065 to 17,531.[27]

Look carefully at these numbers. The 103rd Assembly District had a total of 70,387 registered Republicans. To win the primary, in other words, Molinaro needed to win the support of just four percent of the district's Republican voters. To put it another way, he needed just twenty-six votes in each of the two counties' 104 election districts to win. In the days of the old machine, that was pretty easy: each of the two precinct captains was expected to cast his or her vote for the machine candidate and bring in at least three or four relatives– five plus five each, ten votes without leaving the house, just sixteen more needed to win. Add in a few holders of patronage jobs and their relatives, or maybe friends from the local tavern or coffee shop, and the job was done. If those fairly automatic votes for the old machine are harder to come by in the twenty-first century, the basic math is a constant: find an organizer in each election district who can round up twenty-five or more voters and you're in the game. New Yorkers are not unique in throwing away these key voting rights. Tammy Duckworth won her Democratic primary for the Senate in Illinois with just 26 votes per election district and went on to win in the general election. Lizzie Pannill Fletcher needed just 64 votes per district to win a run-off primary, but more than 800 to beat an incumbent in the 2018 general election for Congress in the 7th district of Texas. There are districts like these throughout the country, for Congress sometimes, for state offices almost always. As much as the parties may "largely nullify each other's effectiveness," in November, in the primaries "the machines have no organized competition. Hence they become enormously effective and, so long as the average voter fails to participate, are practically invincible."[28] The point here, which we will elaborate in Chapter three, is that the decline of the regular party organizations has left a void that can be filled.

The final, and still enduring point that Kent made with regard to primaries, is that "members of the state central committee, control of which is key to the whole machine, are elected in the primaries."[29] Those who charged during or after the 2016 elections that the system is somehow rigged have only their own passivity or ignorance of the process to blame. It is, in a nutshell, folly to register as an independent or join a third party when the major parties are so open to challenge in their primaries.

Even at the national level, looking back to 2016, although there is no hard evidence of DNC interference in the presidential primaries or caucuses, there is no doubt that there was a Clinton bias at the higher levels of the DNC; but whatever the biases various state committees and the national committees may have had, they were there because Democrats– or, more correctly, Democrats who voted in party primaries– put them there. For most of its history the Republican and Democratic National Committees were noteworthy less for their powers than an almost total lack of real influence. The truth is that at the national level (and indeed in most states) the Democratic Party had little presence as an organized entity, and very little influence with Democratic voters. In some states, the state committees held statewide conventions to endorse candidates, but these endorsements were only sporadically effective. Contrary to its name, moreover, the DNC almost never acted as the national headquarters of the party (nor did its Republican counterpart). Their chief and almost exclusive function was that of raising money, mostly from interest groups, to underwrite the national conventions every four years.

This picture has been changing in recent years, particularly in the arena of congressional politics. Supreme Court decisions on campaign finance have freed the national committees from virtually all of the regulations that still limit many individual candidates. Because the national committees have a long history of working with political consultants, competent staff, media experts, fundraisers, and so on, the professionalization of campaigns has uniquely positioned them to offer technical help and advice to selected candidates. "While these resources are found abundantly within the party network, they are difficult to procure elsewhere."[30] The committees have, in particular, developed increasingly sophisticated data banks for their candidates. After his unsuccessful run for President in 2004, former Vermont Governor Howard Dean became chairman of the DNC where he "worked out a deal in which the national party assumed the costs of improving and maintaining the state voter files and building a new data base to house them, in exchange for permission to aggregate and extend them."[31] Through Dean's "Vote-Builder" program, and subsequent targeting models developed by both parties, endorsed candidates have access to continuously updated files of quality data on states and congressional districts. Who controls these valuable lists and how they will be used, as we shall see in chapters two and three, remain contested questions.

Perhaps the most significant changes in the roles of the national committees derive from two decisions of the Supreme Court. The infamous *Citizens United* case magnified the influence of big donors by allowing unlimited, anonymous contributions to Political Action Committees not working with specific campaigns. The too-seldom noticed *McCutcheon v. FEC* said that the Federal Election Commission could not limit the aggregate amount of donations from any given individual to more than one campaign or party organization. Because the limits how much one can give to a single campaign remain in place, but overall limits do not, what many millionaires do is to donate the maximum allowable amount to each of a number of state party organizations that then transfer the money to the national committees which can either spend them directly or retransfer them to individual campaigns. Although these devices effectively avoid disclosure of who is giving how much to whom, it is generally agreed that as much as a third of the money raised in recent years has come from as few as fifty or sixty mega-donors. What has been less frequently observed is the markedly enhanced role this gives the national party organizations in directing the flow of campaign giving. In allocating resources, they would seem obviously to have as their primary goal "ensuring that the right election candidate emerges from the party's nomination process to give the party the best chance of winning a majority of seats in the Senate and the House." [32] Which is what they do. There is growing evidence, however, that they are making these decisions earlier in the election cycle, often picking favorites more than a year in advance, and actively recruiting "attractive candidates." Party leaders insist that this is a collaborative process rather than one of central control. "As a chair," said one state party chair, "I remember walking around often saying

'Where's the backroom? Where's the room where I go to smoke cigars and make all the decisions, because I haven't found the door.'"[33]

They also argue that questions of ideology do not enter into these negotiations. "We're not anti-conservative," said one Republican leader, "We're just anti-people-who-can't-win."[34] In actual fact, there are biases in both parties, some of which stem from sincere beliefs that more moderate candidates are better positioned to win, some from the true preferences of those who serve as party leaders. "At times when politics are polarizing and the parties are moving away from each other ideologically, party leadership may represent yesterday's ideological preferences, which are more moderate."[35] To replace yesterday's leaders it what today's politics is all about. Today's unresolved questions both with regards to money and voter lists will be decided in tomorrow's primary elections for party positions.

One suspects, however, that tensions between national, state, and local party organizations will endure. Were today's progressive Democrats, even those who complain the most about the present "establishment," to take control of the campaign committees, they would probably be just as reluctant to support "moderates" as today's committees are to back "progressives." The true check on over-centralization is to strengthen local parties in their ability to select their own candidates. They must, more importantly, come back in not just for one exciting candidate or campaign, but for the longer haul of building an organizations, new Tammany Halls if you will. Campaign-think is different from movement-think. "It is the job of political consultants and staffers to concern themselves with optics, staging, and their own 'punch lists,' rather than constructing lasting political organizations and grassroots networks;"[36] It is the job of political activists to rebuild those networks.

## The Lessons of 2018

Although they actually lost ground in the Senate, Democrats did very well in 2018, making a net gain of 42 seats in the House and nearly 300 seats (a 4.5% increase) in state legislatures. Although the House gains were important in many senses, this was not the stuff of what pundits call a "wave" election. The party out of power almost always makes gains in mid-term (or non-presidential) election years, and 2018 was no exception. The

42 seats flipped to the Democrats exceeded the historical midterm average of 14, but the shift of 42 seats was fewer than in twelve of twenty-five previous midterms, and the Democratic net loss of two Senate seats pretty much ruined the celebration. What was perhaps more promising was the emergence– in many areas– of an energized Democratic grassroots, a pattern that was replicated in some areas in the few state legislative elections in 2019.

Most of the gains for Democrats in 2018 can be attributed to one factor: turnout. With nearly half (49.2%) of all registered voters actually casting votes in the general election, it was the highest turnout for a midterm election in one hundred years, 12.5% higher than in 2014. All kinds of reported activities, from contacting an elected official, giving money, or posting a political message on the internet, also rose significantly. Most importantly, in terms of this book, the percentage of Democrats who said they had worked in a campaign rose to nine percent, a number that is unusually high. Many of those who said that had worked may have only spent an evening or two at best making phone calls or stuffing envelopes, but there were at least a dozen congressional campaigns and many at the state legislative level where volunteers quite clearly made the difference. Here are a few.

The Democrats surge in voting for the House was led by California where seven incumbent Republicans were replaced by Democrats. In at least four of these contests, a key factor was a new law that legalized a practice now known as "ballot harvesting," in which volunteers were allowed to collect absentee ballots in bulk and bring them to election offices. In North Carolina, which did not have the screening protections that were embodied in the California law, the returns in one House district were overturned partly on the grounds that an illegal form of vote harvesting– where the volunteers not only delivered the ballots but filled them out as well– biased the outcome. There have been no credible charges of this kind in California, but the practice very clearly worked in the Democrats favor. It worked, in a nutshell, because, as one Democratic operative put it, "we out-hustled the other guys." In one Southern California district, 56% of the votes came in after elections day, and the insurgent Democrat, T.J. Cox, who had trailed badly on election night, wound up winning by 862 votes. Whatever else happened in the campaign, the Democrats had to have had an extraordinary ground game in place before Election Day: it takes thousands and thousands of volunteers to "harvest" that many absentee ballots.

There are, at the other extreme, elections that were figuratively "stolen," particularly in primaries. Lizzie Pannill Fletcher was one of seven relatively unknown candidates who entered a Houston area Democratic primary to run against long term incumbent and powerful member of the Appropriations Committee, John Culbertson, in a district rated "Safe to Likely Republican" by most observers. In a relatively low-key primary runoff, Fletcher won the nomination with just 9888 votes, but a series of blunders by the incumbent brought national help to Fletcher and she won rather easily in November.

The most heralded upset of 2018 was that of Alexandria Ocasio-Cortez, a young, virtually unknown candidate who toppled a long-term incumbent and powerhouse in the House Democratic leadership, Joe Crowley. Crowley, focused on his Washington career, ran a relatively lackluster campaign, seldom even visiting his district. Although he spent $3.4 million compared to AOC's $194,000, almost all of it went to staff and cookie-cutter mailings. Ocasio-Cortez targeted– not Latinos, as one might expect in a district nearly half Hispanic– but younger voters, particularly Sanders supporters, in the more gentrified areas of Queens. Avoiding, and even deriding traditional media and direct mail, the campaign ran almost entirely on-line and in person. Digital, said the director of her communications campaign, "is not the future of campaigns, it's the present of campaigning."[37]

While it is tempting to trumpet the AOC campaign as paradigmatic of the emergence of a new, people-oriented politics, some significant caveats are in order. Most importantly, the incumbent Joe Crowley, never having had a significant challenger, and having early polls in hand showing him far ahead in the race, ran a perfunctory campaign. Second, the tendency for New Yorkers not to vote in primaries helped set the bar low for a challenger. With only 13% of registered Democrats going to the polls, Ocasio-Cortez's low-visibility campaign enabled her essentially to "steal" a seat from a sleeping giant. In almost every election cycle, it seems, there is at least one Crowley or Culbertson to let a more energetic challenger pull off a well-earned upset. It is worth noting, finally, that although there was not a huge registration, door-to-door or get-out-the-vote campaign here, there were enough volunteers and enough very sophisticated digital media experts involved to enable AOC's campaign to reach voters under the opposition's political radar. She won with fewer than forty votes per precinct, winning only two election districts with

150 votes or more. There were, in fact, twenty-one districts in which neither candidate won more than ten votes.

An interesting contrast to the Ocasio-Cortez race was the campaign of Alessandra Biaggi in an adjacent State Senate district. The incumbent, Jeffrey Klein, was the leader of the Independent Democratic Conference which had allied with state Republicans to share control of the State Senate. Resentment among labor and liberal Democrats against Klein was strong, and Biaggi was able to attract substantial numbers of volunteers to counter the incumbent's nearly 10-to-1 edge in fund-raising. Her only paid advertising was on social media, but her campaign manager identified 600 on-the ground volunteers who trained with the campaign and began canvassing the district six months before the election.[38] The result was a primary victory with 19,318 votes, *nearly three thousand more votes than AOC garnered in a congressional district more than twice the size of Biaggi's state senate district.*[39]

The power of volunteers was also evident in three congressional races that flipped to the Democrats in 2018, Antonio Delgado, in New York's 19th congressional district, Tom Malinowski in New Jersey's 7th and Kendra Horn in Oklahoma's 5th. In a sense, all three ran relatively conventional campaigns using a full range of media, attracting support (and opposition) from the parties' national committees as well as independent expenditures from political action committees. What distinguished these races were their ground games. Delgado won the Democratic nomination in a seven-person primary in large part by substantially outspending his rivals and proving a formidable debater in a series of candidate forums held throughout the sprawling Hudson Valley district. Two of his opponents, especially a 27-year-old political novice named Gareth Rhodes, built their campaigns almost entirely on door-to-door volunteers who largely came over to the Delgado campaign for the general election. The "persuasion effects" of volunteers— how much they can change people's candidate preferences– are difficult to measure; but what door-to-door campaigns are good at is registering new voters, increasing the turnout of supporters, and harvesting absentee ballots. The numbers in this district were quite remarkable.

Let's start with turnout. In 2016, Congressman Faso was opposed by Zephyr Teachout, a well-funded Democrat who had achieved considerable name recognition in a 2014 run for Governor in the Democratic primary. She lost 141,224 to Faso's 166,171, a margin of 24, 947 votes or 46% to 54%.

Delgado beat Faso in 2018 by 15,000, 147,873 to 132,873 or 52.3% to 47.7%. Antipathy to President Trump, Faso's stand on health care issues, his refusal to hold town meetings, and an incredibly inept television commercial funded by the Republican Congressional Campaign Committee,[40] contributed to this switch, but the pattern is interesting. Voter turnout in non-presidential years is typically off by anywhere from ten to twenty percent, averaging a fall-off of 13.5% from 2002 through 2018. The fall-off for Faso was bigger than average at 20.6%, but the Democratic vote for Delgado was a remarkable 6000 votes higher than Teachout's, an *increase* of almost ten percent. Arguably, much of what Delgado gained was from voters switching from the Republican to the Democrat, but switches of that magnitude are unusual and there are local data that suggest otherwise. In Columbia County (where I live), for example, between 2016 and 2018 the percentage of registered Democrats increased by 15.9% as compared with an increase in all other parties of just 6.4%. In my little town of Copake, 60 volunteers registered 209 Democrats, an increase of 27.5% compared with a Republican increase of 32 (3.6%).

The patterns in northern New Jersey were similar. After winning the Democratic primary to take on 10-Year incumbent Leonard Lance, Tom Malinowski, like Antonio Delgado, ran a volunteer campaign in parallel with a more traditional media campaigns. And like Delgado, Malinowski increased the Democratic vote from 2016 by 12.7% while the vote on the Republican line fell by 13.5%. As with Delgado, moreover, part of the explanation for the Democrats improved performance was a registration drive that increased the number of Democratic registrants by more than ten percent.

And finally, there is the case of Oklahoma's 5th district where Democrat Kendra Horn narrowly defeated a Republican incumbent who had won his seat by more than 20% just two years before. The Horn campaign was a model of the kind of election effort that we will describe in greater detail in this book, especially in the ways in which door-to-door, digital and media campaigns were layered on top of each other. As with many of the volunteers in Malinowski's campaign, the proximate roots of their involvement was the January 2018 Women's March on Washington where a small group of dedicated activists came home to mobilize their friends. In the suburbs north of Oklahoma City, 350 volunteers were mobilized within a few months providing the Horn campaign with a ready base when she won the primary.

In the more urban part of the district, volunteers were recruited largely from the University and groups like Planned Parenthood in which Horn had been active. When classes began in September, some of the student volunteers were given small stipends to continue their work if only because the campaign found that the young students were not only effective but served as an important motivating force. They were also given seminars, tours of the capital, guest speakers and socials. With more than 2000 completed shifts, the Horn campaign had the largest volunteer operation in the state.

Most importantly, little volunteer time was wasted. "If you walk into to do something you've never done before," said campaign manager Ward Curtin, "the campaign better be organized."[41] So those who were uncomfortable going door-to-door were put to work on social media or direct mail, volunteers were targeted by neighborhood proximity and peer-to-peer contacts. Even some of the campaigns radio, television and print ads were essentially produced by volunteers with media experience. As with Delgado and Malinowski, the outcome was fueled by voters who switched parties and a 17% surge in Democratic votes compared with a decline of 26% for Congressman Russell.

These three districts were notable for extraordinary levels of volunteer activity. Far more sophisticated statistical and demographic analysis would be needed to show that the correlations with increased turnout and Democratic success in these districts are not spurious, but the overall pattern is persuasive and consistent with on-the-ground expert experience. Check these numbers:

|  | All Congressional Districts | NY 19 | NJ 7 | OK 5 |
|---|---|---|---|---|
| Change in Democratic Vote Total, 2016-18 | - 1.9% | + 9.7% | +12.7% | +17.3% |
| Change in Republican Vote Total, 2016-18 | -20.3% | - 20.3% | -13.5% | -26.4% |

With variations, the pattern is clearly one in which the Republican incumbents suffered from what were essentially average fall-offs in participation, while the Democrats benefitted from unusually large surges in total votes, with the increases largest in those districts where volunteer efforts were best organized and most robust. Turnout was certainly not the only variable of importance in any of these races: all three Democrats clearly switched a number of voters who had supported Republicans just two years before. But the Democratic gains in these districts– considerably greater than the national average– are striking.

Putting people back in politics, bringing campaigns back into the streets, works. In 2018 the campaigns that emphasized field work were the ones most likely to succeed. The ability of volunteers to persuade their neighbors to change their party preferences may or may not have been a factor; their ability to register new voters, to increase turnout, and to make sure– though absentee ballots– that people did not forget to vote was often decisive.

The philosopher Emmanuel Kant's categorical imperative suggests that the moral foundation of good society begins with treating other people as ends not means. It begins with relating to others as real people not abstractions. To the extent that the modern political campaign packages voters it is morally deficient. To the extent that it manipulates symbols of enmity and division it dehumanizes our politics. Putting people back in politics is a moral imperative. It is also smart politics.

# Endnotes

1   Gary W. Reichard, Deadlock and Disillusionment: American Politics since 1968 (Malden, MA: John Wiley and Sons, 2016), 334.

2   Robert Stefan Foa and Yascha Mounk, "The Democratic Discontent," 27 Journal of Democracy (July 2016), 6.

3   Ibid. 9.

4   Alexis de Tocqueville's Democracy in America is available in a number of formats. Robert D. Putnam, Bowling Alone: The Collapse and Revival of American Community (New York: Simon and Schuster, 2000).

5   Amy Widestrom, Displacing Democracy: Economic Segregation in America (Philadelphia: University of Pennsylvania Press, 2015), 5.

6   Ibid. 183.

7   Zoltan Hajnal, Nazita Najevardi and Lindsay Nielson, "Voter Identification Laws and the Suppression of Minority Votes," 79 Journal of Politics (April 2017), 363-79.

8   Special Memo, Gerrymandering Increasingly Defies the Will of Voters (Washington: National Committee for an Effective Congress, May, 2017).

9   These figures, and some of those which follow, are derived from exit polls as reported in Larry J. Sabato, "The 2016 Election That Broke All, or At Least Most of the Rules," Larry J. Sabato, Kyle Kondik and Geoffrey Skelley, Trumped: the 2016 Election That Broke All of the Rules (Lanham, MD: Rowman and Littlefield, 2017), pp. 24-27.

10  Quoted in Conor Lynch, "Neoliberalism's Epic Fall," accessed May9, 2017 at http://www.salon.com/2016/11/19/neoliberalisms-epic-fail-the-reaction-to-hillary-clintons-loss-exposed-the-impotent-elitism-of-liberalism

11  Donald M. Shea and Michael John Burton, Campaign Craft: The Strategies, Tactics, and Art of Political Campaign Management (Westport, CT: Praeger, 3rd ed., 2006), 10-11.

12  Early polls can also be vital in their capacity to convince potential donors that a candidate is viable and thus worthy of financial support. Some party organizations also require aspiring candidates to submit poll data for the same reason.

13  The more highly educated the voters, the more likely they are to respond. The education gap in 2016 was unusually strong which is probably why so many pollsters failed to take it into account. See Nate Cohen, "A 2016 Review: Why Key State Polls Were Wrong About Trump," The New York Times, May 31, 2017, A25.

14  On these forms of what they call "actualizing citizenship" see W. Lance Bennett, Deen Freelon and Chris Wells, "Changing Citizen Identity and the Rise of a Participatory Media Culture," in Lonnie R. Sherrod, Judith Torney-Purta and Constance A Flanagan, Handbook of Research on Civic Engagement in Youth (Hoboken, NJ: John Wiley and Sons, 2010), 393-423.

15 Pippa Norris, "The Evolution of Election Campaigns: Eroding Political Engagement?" paper published by the Harvard University School of Government, January 17, 2004, available at hks.Harvard.edu/fs/pnorris/Acrobat/Otago/The/Evolution/of/Election/Campaigns.pdf, 7.

16 Shea and Burton, 12

17 The National Council of State Legislatures compiles these figures every two years. In 2015-16, 260 of (48.6%) members of Congress had served previously in a state legislature.

18 Daniel Kreiss, Prototype Politics: Technology-Intensive Campaigning and the Data of Democracy (New York: Oxford University Press, 2016), 219.

19 Eitan D. Hersh, Hacking the Electorate: How Campaigns Perceive Voters (New York: Cambridge University Press, 2015), 7.

20 Theda Skocpol, The Missing Middle: Working Families and the Future of American Social Policy (New York: The Century Foundation, 2000), 167.

21 Daniel Kreiss, Taking Our Country Back: The Crafting of Networked Politics from Howard Dean to Barak Obama (New York: Oxford University Press, 2012), 23.

22 Quoted in ibid. 27.

23 See Robert K. Merton's classic essay, "The Latent Functions of the Machine: A Sociologist's View," in Merton, Social Theory and Social Structure (Glencoe, IL: The Free Press, 1957), 75. This classic essay, together with a rich assortment of cases studies and analytic essays can be found in Alexander B. Callow, Jr., The City Boss in America: An Interpretive Reader (New York: Oxford University Press, 1976). Arguably the best, and certainly the most fun to read, of the many case studies of individual machines is Milton Rakove, Don't Make No Waves. . . Don't Back No Losers: An Insiders' Analysis of the Daley Machine (Bloomington: Indiana University Press, 1976).

24 Frank R. Kent, The Great Game of Politics (Garden City, NY: Doubleday, Doran and Co., 1933), 11.

25 Ibid. 10.

26 A growing number of states have open primary laws that allow voters to cast ballots in the contests of parties in which they are not enrolled; but in sixteen you must be registered with a party to vote in its primary, and in another ten there are significant limits on switching

27 Edward V. Schneier, John Brian Murtaugh and Antoinette Pole, New York Politics: A Tale of Two States (Armonk, NY: M, E. Sharpe, 2010), 74.

28 Kent, 10.

29 Ibid. 11.

30 Hans J. G. Hassell, The Party's Primary: Control of Congressional Nominations (New York: Cambridge University Press, 2018), 190.

31 Kreiss, Prototype Politics, 9.

32  Hassell, 14.

33  Quoted in ibid., 45.

34  Ibid., 46,

35  Ibid., 188.

36  Heather Gautney, Crashing the Party: From the Bernie Sanders Campaign to a Progressive Movement (New York: Verso, 2018), 133.

37  As quoted in Grace Segers, "How Alexandria Ocasio-Cortez Really Won," City and State New York (July 1, 2018), 6.

38  Interview with Ward Curtin, April 3, 2019.

39  Unless otherwise noted, the election figures cited here and in the rest of this section are taken from the official websites of the various relevant state, county, and municipal boards of elections.

40  The commercial showed Delgado, who is black, in a picture from his college days as an aspiring rap musician. Questioning his patriotism and ties to the district it ended by saying "he is not like us." The New York Times accused the campaign of "race baiting," and one local newspaper actually withdrew its endorsement of the Congressman.

41  Interview with Ward Curtin, March 25, 2019.

# Chapter 2

# Putting People Back in Politics

## Executive Summary

It is not easy. Many of us, hardly know our neighbors and seldom range beyond conversations about the weather. Getting people effectively into politics involves a great deal more. For those averse to going door to door, there is work to be done; but the surest and most cost-effective way to make a difference is through face-to-face communication. Campaign professionals have important roles to play, as does the money that pays them; but unless and until there are organized and enduring links between candidates and voters the real impact of the 2020 election– as much as it may mark a turning point in our politics– will not be realized.

Political change begins by locating yourself in the fractured world of state, local and national institutions. In the days of machine politics, when most voters cast straight ticket ballots, the goal was a "balanced" slate of candidates from each significant ethnic group, neighborhood, and so on. Without strong parties, cooperation between state, local, district, and national campaigns are problematic. Candidates and volunteers alike are confronted with decisions, often unavoidable, as to how much and with whom to work. Particularly sticky situations arise in the wake of divisive primaries. The solution, easier to state than to effectuate is to create enduring organizations and coalitions that cut across the artificial boundaries of local, regional and– ultimately– state lines.

By winning control of the House in 2018, the Democrats were able to begin fleshing out an agenda for change, but the list of things they have been unable to do is far longer and more significant. A Democratic President can and almost certainly will reverse most of the executive orders issued by President Trump. A slim majority in the Senate, combined with continuing control of the House could produce policy changes on the environment, taxes, some spending priorities and perhaps immigration; but unless there is a massive realigning election, most major programs from the "Green New Deal" to health care reform, are unlikely to go very far. With a conservative Supreme Court, and one in every four circuit court judges a Trump appointee, moreover, issues like campaign finance reform will almost certainly languish.

The point here is not simply to diminish expectations, but to underscore the need to view 2020 as a milestone not a goal. It involves the need to realign the dynamics of electoral politics by bringing millions of new voters into the political arena. Democrats in several states in the 1950s and 60s organized robust networks of political clubs that revitalized the party but proved impossible to sustain; but the tools available for successful interpersonal campaigns are far more sophisticated today than they were then, putting a sustainable era of reform very much within reach. The lines of conflicts dividing the parties are changing, though the shape of the coming realignment is by no means clear. It is up to this generation of voters and volunteers to shape it.

## Getting Started

The first step in organizing is to locate yourself politically. Most Americans elect local officials in town, city, county or parish governments; state legislators; a Governor and– in most states– statewide officials such as Attorneys General. Judges, sheriffs, clerks and coroners may run at town, county or state levels. School boards districts often cross town and county lines, and most states have special districts for water, fire, irrigation, flood control, street lights or libraries.

The more local the race the more partisanship and ideology take a back seat to personality and accessibility. And the more you move from general governing bodies— whether local, state or national— to special agencies like library, water and school boards, the less the issues that divide people coincide with those that divide people in state and national elections. The higher the office, conversely, the more its politics becomes entangled with others. Almost every candidate for state or national office, and almost every political volunteer must find ways of cooperating, coexisting with, or avoiding other campaigns.

In the days of the machine, straight-ticket voting was common. It declined in the 1960s, 70s and 80s, replaced by what political scientists called candidate-centered-campaigns. A popular book at the time, *The Party's Over,* by journalist David Broder, argued that parties were becoming increasingly irrelevant, pushed aside by self-starting (usually wealthy) individuals, interest groups and political action committees.[1] But as party lines have tightened, fewer voters, especially at the national level, are voting for individuals rather than parties. Indeed the 2016 elections were the first in modern history in which every state elected a senator of the same party as its presidential choice. What this indicates in specific terms for 2020 is not obvious. Local factors, strong candidates and well-organized campaigns played important roles in 2018, but the looming presence of Donald Trump is what brought many Democratic voters to the polls and the lines of partisan cleavage have grown sharper yet in the battle over impeachment. The massive incompetence displayed by the Republican majorities controlling both houses of Congress gave the out-party Democrats an added advantage in 2018, and a do-nothing Senate may work in their favor again, One telling indicator of Republican problems was and is found in the number and quality of candidates prepared to run against incumbent members of the House and Senate. Near record numbers of Republican incumbents retired in 2018 rather than face uphill campaigns, and the same process is occurring in 2019-20. But it is still an uphill road. As a general rule, incumbents who run for reelection win, their re-election rate in the House has dipped below 90% only twice since 1974. Senators, with six year terms, are only slightly more vulnerable, with more than 80% typically reelected.

While these factors point in a positive direction for Democrats in 2020, they pose challenges as well. Most House all Senate districts encompass numerous counties or assembly districts that each have their own organizations and favorites. There are few mechanisms through which these diverse constituencies can cooperate with the result that costly primary elections both sap resources and impede general election campaigns. Smelling blood in the water, there were a number of districts in mid-2017 in which more than half a dozen candidates had already announced their 2018 candidacies. And there is every indication that this is happening again in 2019-20. Although it is not clear whether divisive primaries are harmful, if only because there is no good way to measure just *how* divisive a primary is, it does seem that the higher the visibility of the race the more negative the effects.[2] Some studies suggest that divisive primaries can actually give a bounce to the winner, largely by increasing name recognition; but these appear to be exceptions to the rule. If nothing else, primaries sap money and volunteer energies that detract from the November effort. They are, as we have noted, the arena in which grassroots campaigns are most effective, but the trick is to make sure that the factions come together to work as hard for the ultimate party candidate in November. Despite Senator Sander's efforts in 2016 to rally his forces behind Clinton, the tendency of many of his supporters to stay home or vote for a third party candidate was a major factor in Trump's victory, and more than one Republican held onto his or her district because warring Democrats were unable to unite.

Even at the local or state legislative level it is never too early to begin a campaign. By the first of the year, almost every serious candidate will have some kind of organization. There are also a number of groups– many organized for the 2018 mid-term cycle– that connect with campaigns. The largest of these, Indivisible, is effectively organized in more than 300 congressional districts in every state and many loosely affiliated local chapters. In a small district, if an organization in your area has yet to coalesce, the first step, in local races, is to become familiar with the election calendar and such necessary tasks as filing for candidacy, holding caucuses (in some states), filing petitions, and reporting campaign finances. It is also important to check local laws: two of my friends in California spent an afternoon in jail for violating a noise ordinance in a town where I had sent them with a sound truck. They didn't think it was funny. Nor would your candidate find it funny if fined for putting up lawn signs in a town that prohibits them more than thirty days before an election. One of the reasons organization is important is to have people who know how to do these things, and in a district of substantial size it will probably require professional help. Given the complex rules of reporting, the ability to organize volunteers, to develop media strategies and coordinate them with other aspects of the campaign, the days of the amateur campaign are largely gone

Absent professional help, your local Board of Elections has lists (often accessible on line) of registered voters. In thirty-one states voters can register by party, and in eleven others they must declare their party identification when (and if) they cast a primary ballot. In all fifty states, precinct by precinct records are available that show how many people voted for candidates of each party in their neighborhood. Usually you can get what is called a walking list that lists registered voters in numerical street order, so if you walk down Elm Street and see that there are voters at numbers 17 and 19, but none at 18, try to sign them up. Candidates, armed with these lists, can go door-to-door on their own in a small community, but even there it will be far more meaningful when done with an organization is in place to coordinate activities and provide continuity with previous volunteer efforts. The mechanisms for keeping what local groups there are in touch with each other across congressional district or state lines are even more fragile. The highly targeted and effective network of volunteers created by Barak Obama in 2008 and expanded in 2012 showed how this can be done. But this network too was short lived and impossible for Hilary Clinton to revive or recreate. There is nothing new about this, and there is a sense in which every campaign must essentially invent itself; but, particularly at the national or statewide level the decline of the old party organizations has left a void that needs to be filled. The key problem of the Democratic Party in most parts of the country is the absence not the strength of a pre-existing network of local organizations willing and able to connect candidates and voters that the groundwork of one campaign can serve as a foundation for the next. Local organizations can and will be divided in 2020 as to who should be the party's candidate for president, but it is important to understand the importance of recognizing that there are larger battles to be fought. Nothing serves better to bring warring factions together than regular face to face meetings and dialogue.

# What Is at Stake in 2020?

Political scientists have used the term "realigning elections" to define electoral cycles in which the demographic groups supporting the parties change significantly. Classic cases include the election of Andrew Jackson 1832, Abraham Lincoln in 1860 and, perhaps most dramatically, Franklin Roosevelt in 1932. Whether defined in terms of specific elections or "realigning periods," what marks these cycles are lasting changes in voting behavior that affect both houses of the Congress as well as the White House. After three Republican landslides in 1920, 24 and 28, Franklin Roosevelt not only won by a landslide in 1932, but the Democrats swept into control of both houses of Congress as well, going from 38% of the House in 1928 to 72% in 1932, and from 41% in the Senate to 62% just four years later. The so-called "New Deal Coalition" held sway for a generation, keeping Democrats in control of the House and Senate for all but the two years following World War II. Only the popular war hero, Dwight Eisenhower was able to break a string of what would have been thirty-six years of Democrats in the White House. What followed in the 1960's was more of a realigning period rather than a single defining election. Lyndon Johnson's successful push for civil rights legislation helped swing African-Americans overwhelmingly into the Democratic Party even as it turned the white South from solidly Democratic to Republican. The change in the south, as is typical in political realignments, came in stages, starting in 1964 when Republican Barry Goldwater carried four states of the old Confederacy that had been reliably Democratic for nearly a century. All but two of the Senate seats in those thirteen states, and 96 of 120 House seats remained in Democratic hands. Not until 1994 would a majority of the Senators and Representatives from these states be Republicans. Today, the states of the old Confederacy are as solidly Republican as they once were Democratic with all but two United States Senators in Republican hands, and both houses of the state legislature in 12 of the 13 states Republican. Meanwhile the northeast, once the most solid base of Republican voters, turned increasingly Democratic as did the Pacific coast, making a political map of the country today almost a mirror of what it was in 1960.

When Newt Gingrich led the Republican takeover of the House in 1994, the contours of a revised alignment were defined. With only wisps of the

New Deal coalition still in the air, a tenuous Republican era has emerged in which they have controlled the House for 36 for the past 42 years, and the Senate for 32. While the essential voting blocs of the past remained constant, the balance tipped toward the Republicans with the emergence of a new set of "social issues" added to the list. Although Donald Trump has scrambled some of these patterns, the relative positions of the two parties have been stable. Trump's 2016 road to victory, in fact, traveled a path remarkably similar to Mitt Romney's losing effort in 2012. Trump and Romney both won every southern state save Virginia, but Trump carried Florida which Romney had lost. The results west of the Mississippi were identical, save in Iowa where Clinton lost a state that Obama had won. The northeast was solidly Democratic in both elections, except in Pennsylvania. The shifts that decided the election were in the Great Lakes area where Trump flipped Ohio, Michigan and Wisconsin. Polling data also point to less significant shifts than many pundits have suggested took place. Thus, although Trump trailed Clinton by 12% among women, Romney had trailed Obama by 11. Turnout among African-Americans and younger voters was appreciably higher in 2012 than 2016, but both groups were solidly Democratic. Finally, the white working-class explanation for the Trump victory– if only because of its dramatic effects in the crucial states of the Great Lakes region– is only partially supported by the data. There was an increase in turnout, particularly among "non-Hispanic whites who worked as farmers, ranchers, or other agricultural workers," that faded in 2018. Whether the 2016 surge was the product of "the 'working class' or the 'white' portion of the group identity" remains subject to debate;[3] but the most remarkable thing about Trump's victory is how unremarkable it was. In a variety of statistical studies, virtually all of the state-by-state variance in the 2016 vote is predicted by just three variables: historic patterns of party voting, the Romney vote in 2012, and the percentage of white non-college graduates in the population.

The 2018 elections enabled the Democrats to retake the House of Representatives largely through selective increases in turnout. For Democrats, the most interesting change was the continuing movement of better educated voters toward the Party. As recently as the early 1990s, Republicans had almost a 15% edge among college graduates; in 2018 Democrats had a comparable lead. Among whites who never completed high school, conversely, a 5 to 8% Democratic advantage has shifted to a small margin favorable to the G. O. P., much of this in rural areas. The Democrats' growing appeal to college-educated voters was particularly strong among suburban women. And Democrats continue to lead among minority voters, not just African-Americans, but increasingly among Hispanics and Asians. Finally, the gap between urban and rural voters continues to widen, with a 25 to 30 percent Democratic edge in cities, and a growing Republican margin in rural areas.[4] Despite these movements, the bottom line moving into 2020 is the relative absence of any single electoral indicator of significant realignment. For twenty years or more, national elections have been decided more in terms of relatively small variations in turnout than changes in preference; but if voters have not significantly changed their electoral preferences, differences over issues have diverged quite dramatically. The most sophisticated and accurate predictions of presidential voting in the late twentieth century were founded in economics: higher wages, lower unemployment rates and similar indicator were highly correlated with the success or failure of the incumbent presidents and their parties. Yet despite a rising stock market and declining unemployment, neither Obama nor Trump earned points from the voters. Trump's approval ratings remained mired in the same 38-43% range virtually from the day he took office. Generic polls of party preferences for the House have been even more stable, showing a persistent average Democratic advantage of four to seven percent. In demographic terms, the bases of the two parties have been in a state of what we might call "stable polarization." Instead of realignment what the past three decades have seen are gradually shifting patterns of preference and intensity. As one major study put it, "the 2016 elections continue to reflect electoral alignments wet in motion by a critical era that occurred nearly a half century ago."[5]

Many years ago, political scientist E. E. Schattschneider argued that electoral realignments were founded in what he called the displacement of conflict. "The outcome of the game of politics depends on which of a multitude of possible conflicts gains the dominant position:" those who can define what we fight about can also decide who wins and loses.[6] What Schattschneider failed to recognize was the staying power of the old order. In the 1990's, the walls of Bill Clinton's campaign offices were covered with signs (lest anyone forgot) reminding all that "It's the economy stupid!" And it was. In 1992 and throughout most of the period a majority of voters polled by Gallup ranked economic issues as first in importance. In 2018 the percentage of voters putting economic issues at the top in 2018 reached an all-time low of just 12%. Instead of promoting changes in the nature of conflict, today's Republican and Democratic campaigns alike are defining the key issues essentially in the same terms as in the 1990s with Democrats, even "progressives," essentially emphasizing elaborations on New Deal liberalism and Republicans continuing to rail against big governments and keeping their evangelical base in line on social issues. Although the current lines of partisan conflict are hopelessly out of date, both parties seem at best conflicted about a change in direction, making the mismatch between parties and voters large and growing. There is nothing really new in such a seeming disjunction between party positions and voter concerns. Electoral realignments are almost invariably discovered after the fact. Lincoln in 1860 made almost no mention of slavery and never spoke of abolition, focusing almost entirely on unifying the Republican Party. Roosevelt's campaign in 1932 offered few hints of his coming economic reforms.

It does seem, however, as if the struggle to redefine the scope of conflict has already begun in the Republican Party where the "establishment," with varying degrees of vigor, has resisted the President's repeated attempts to emphasize an us-versus-them struggle between demographic groups. In its early 2019 Gallup surveys, immigration ranked most important among Republicans with as many as 41%, as compared with just 5% of Democrats, numbers that probably explain why Trump has been so insistent on playing to his ethnic cards. While many of the Party's more traditional economic conservatives are uncomfortable with these appeals, most of them are too happy with their tax cuts, regulatory "reforms," and overall economic policies to vote Democratic. Other issues on which there are hints of widening gaps in public attitudes between Republicans and Democrats are climate change, Russian influence, good government, the treatment of women and income inequality, seldom mentioned by candidates of either party in 2018 or in the early debates among the Democrats running for President in 2020. Despite the importance many Democratic voters placed on these issues, nearly two-thirds of all television commercials for Democratic candidates in 2018 were about health. This fact that this was the number one campaign issue in 2018 is interesting in its own right, but also insofar as it may reflect some emerging splits among Democrats on these other issues. For as much as issues like climate change divide Democrats from Republicans, they also play differently among younger and older supporters within the Democratic electorate. Income inequality, a hot button issue for younger voters and minorities, may not inspire suburban women. And the "issues" of foreign campaign interference and the functioning of our government institutions are largely in the category of what professionals call "inside baseball," fascinating to policy wonks and political scientists, but unlikely to interest many others. As with immigration and minority rights, it is strategically more prudent to hope that the Republicans themselves will go down in flames by defining key issues in these terms. And there is some evidence that this is actually happening. "President Trump's endorsements," as one study of the 2018 elections showed, "may be doing little to elicit engagement from voters on the Republican side, whilst creating a rallying effect around opposing candidates and increasing engagement among Democratic voters. The story then from these findings may be one of presidential backlash rather than presidential coattails."[7] How the impeachment is will affect these numbers– aside from their obvious effect of intensifying partisan divisions is anybody's guess.

The shifts that may prove most important in 2020 are those that point toward increasingly different electoral strategies for the two parties. Four demographic patterns are particularly significant. First, although record numbers of those between the ages of 18 and 29 voted in 2018, their turnout rate of just over 30% is far below that of their seniors. The enhanced participation of younger voters is absolutely crucial to the future of the Democratic Party. This is the group, moreover, that is probably least effectively reached by traditional campaigns. Second, urban and suburban voters in the thirteen largest metropolitan areas elect nearly one-third of all members of the House of Representatives. These congressional districts are in media markets that extend over six or more congressional districts, virtually pricing mass media out of the picture (every television ad, for example, aimed at one district must pay for five or more). Third, the most reliably Democratic ethnic groups– Blacks, Hispanics, and Asians– are least likely to register and vote. And finally, despite Trump's ability to cut into working class constituencies, the lowest 20% of income earners remain almost 20% more likely to vote Democratic. Especially in urban areas, these potential voters also have unusually low percentages of participation in electoral politics.

The bottom line is relatively simple. The areas of greatest Republican strength– white, rural, more affluent, older– are those in which traditional media campaigns are most cost-effective. They are also the kinds of districts most suited to the Republican's greater fund-raising ability. Whatever chances Democrats have in these districts lie in finding pockets of potential support, getting them registered and getting them out to vote without simultaneously awakening more dormant conservatives. Media campaigns in these districts will almost invariably be more than matched by outside groups and will serve largely to arouse otherwise quiescent Republicans. In the suburbs, the key for the Democrats involves the kind of targeted effort, described in Chapter 1, of people like Delgado in New York, Malinowski in New Jersey and Hall in Oklahoma.

The dynamics of political change are founded in mobilization not conversion. The running argument between "progressive" and "mainstream" Democrats largely misses the point. With the exception of the major shift among white voters in the South, most electoral realignments in America have derived from shifts in who voted rather than how. Roosevelt's victory in 1932 had its roots in Al Smith's ability four years earlier to bring first and second generation, largely Catholic workers into the electorate. The Republican resurgence of the 1990s was fueled in large part by a massive flow of previously apolitical white evangelicals into the Republican Party and blending them into an alliance of convenience with the Party's more affluent base. To again become the dominant party, the Democrats must similarly mobilize young voters and minorities without losing their educated and working class bases. To do this will take hard work more than a change in message as there is no single issue that will sustain the party's growing appeal to suburban women in California, its hold on African Americans in Alabama, and young people throughout the country. The issues such as climate change that matters to these groups are of little interest to most Republicans. If this is to prove a period of political realignment, it will not involve the conversion of Trump's hard core.

## The Long Road to Reform

The road to change is long. Significant reform depends on winning the Presidency, retaining and extending a Democratic majority in the House, and changing the Senate sufficiently to control its agenda. In the somewhat longer run, it involves changes in state legislatures to reverse laws restricting the right to vote; and finally it goes to the federal courts and perhaps even to amending the Constitution. Only then is there a realistic prospect of changes in campaign finance rules, and in most major areas of public policy. Looking first at what we can hope for in 2020, the absolute first priority is simply that of sustaining and consolidating the gains of 2018. Its unprecedented levels of community activism can all too easily slide back into sloth and despair. Most of the forty newly elected moderate and progressive members of the House should have the advantages of incumbency, and, if they are smart, the cadres of volunteers and lists of voters who, in many cases, made their victories possible. In many districts, however, the gains of 2018 will dissipate in dissolution: its organization disbanded, its records lost and volunteers dispersed. This is why organizations that last beyond campaigns are so important.

Despite Democratic successes in 2018, there is still low hanging fruit on the tree. The flood of Republican retirements that left 25 House and three Senate seats vacant going into 2018 is continuing into 2020. Many of these retirements are those of moderates torn between fear of primary election threats from the right and of Democratic challenges in November. Fifty-three House Republicans won their 2018 races by less than ten percent. The situation in the Senate is more difficult. While it is better than in 2018 when Democrats were defending 26 of 35 seats, in 2020 the 22 Republican seats (of 34) are mostly in deep red states. There are Republican seats that Democrats can win, but their ability to attract strong candidates has been limited. It will require effective campaigns and a Democratic surge to prevent Mitch McConnell from using the slenderest of majorities to deploy a replay of his successful attempt to block Democratic policies and appointments. "Democrats could win the immediate fight against Donald Trump in 2020 but lose the larger battle against the Republican Party that supported and enabled him."[8]

Nor is the Trump/Pence coalition as vulnerable as national polls might make it appear. Such is the map of the Electoral College that most experts agree that the Democrats must win the popular vote by at least three or four percent in order to overcome its distorting affects. And in the key swing states, Trump's approval ratings have been consistently higher than in national polls. Even if Democrats win the presidency, expand their control of the House and win the Senate, the distance between cup and lip will remain frustratingly large. There will be a number of Democratic Senators who, rightly or wrongly, whether out of conviction or political perspectives on their constituencies, will join with the Republicans in blocking a number of legislative initiatives. A Democratic President can, and almost certainly will, undo many of Trump's executive orders on climate change, public lands, immigration, health care, and foreign policy, and perhaps even extend some of Obama's initiatives. And if there is a Democratic surge, they might be able to overcome the resistance of Senate Republicans and enact modest legislative changes in tax and spending policies, health care, and environmental protection. With reapportionment on every state's agenda in 2021, moreover, state legislatures are increasingly important. Every legislative district, state and national must be redrawn in 2021. More is at stake in 2020, in other words, then Congress and the Presidency. Here again the odds are long. Democrats go into 2020 with control of both houses and the governorship in only six states compared with more than fifteen for the Republicans.

The growth of intra-party polarization is growing in both parties It is likely that we will see a significant number of insufficiently conservative incumbent Republicans and insufficiently progressive Democrats challenged in primaries, some successfully. The key question is whether and how much these divisions will effect general election outcomes. Whether Alabama Republicans, by again nominating the disastrous Roy Moore will allow Democrat Doug Jones to again win in a deeply red state is up in the air, as is the question of whether moderate and progressive Democrats can work together when the activist base is considerably to the left of the party's voters. Certainly, the President's success in getting some Democrats to fight amongst each other than against him is discouraging at best. Polarization is nationalizing politics to the point at it may no longer be true that "all politics is local," but being a Democrats is Queens is still not the same as it is in Kansas.

Both parties' national campaign committees have become increasingly active in recruiting candidates, and some state committees are similarly involved. While these efforts come with the promise of financial and professional help, they are not always sensitive to local issues and personalities. And they are not particularly likely to seek out candidates who appeal to younger voters or who are significantly more liberal. This is why local organizations are so much needed. Campaigns run from outside of the district bind them into patterns of activity and methods of campaigning that, as argued in Chapter 1 are increasingly less effective and often counterproductive.

Although party loyalties have hardened, there are crucially large numbers of voters who can be influenced if volunteers build on their 2018 successes. The very real question is whether today's activists have the stamina to create a new politics of reform. There are precedents. In California in the 1950s, a system known as cross-filing allowed anyone to run in either party's primary, and prohibited party endorsements. My friend, Democrat Steve Zetterburg, ran against a well-funded lawyer named Richard Nixon. With party labels absent, voters were often confused. The Nixon campaign's many billboards mentioned no party affiliation. Every night, Zetterburg volunteers posted a strip saying "Republican" between the lines "Vote for Richard Nixon" and "for Congress," and every morning Republican volunteers would paste a plain strip of paper blocking it out. By Election Day, the line was an inch think. Nixon won both party's primaries. Reform Democrats in California evaded this system by forming local "clubs," not part of the formal party and thus able to make primary endorsements. The clubs coalesced into the California Democratic Council of Clubs that began to endorse on a statewide level. Similarly, in New York, the reform Democrats who replaced Tammany leader Carmine DeSapio helped organize a New York Democratic Coalition of clubs (NDC) that became a major player, particularly in the city. When I ran for Congress in 1976, the core of my campaign was the NDC-affiliated Chelsea, West Village, Downtown, Gay and Lesbian, and Staten Island clubs whose endorsements made me the "official" progressive candidate. The CDC, NDC and groups such as the Independent Voters of Illinois remained influential throughout the 1970s, and still have local pockets of power. In their day, they reformed party rules, elected progressive candidates and invigorated the Democratic Party. They were also, in the words of Tammany's Boss Plunkitt, "mornin' glories– looked lovely in the mornin' and withered up in a short time."[9] In a sense, the clubs were victims of their own success: once elected with club help, incumbent politicians grew increasingly wary of the sometimes "radical" clubs. Reform comes in cycles: elect a Pat Brown, a Mario Cuomo, and thoughtful, progressive members of the House and Senate, and. . . the organizational imperative fades into the sunset. How to rebuild and sustain such a movement for change is the dominant issue of our times. Beyond 2020 it needs the kind of infrastructure that organizations like the CDC provided. In most areas what is left of the regular organizations will probably join happily into a movement to revive the party.

A shortcoming of the club movement was that much of its organizing energy was generated in relatively affluent communities that were largely Republican. Through their state councils the reformers could be a significant factor in statewide Democratic primaries, and in local races in more affluent, liberal areas like Hollywood and Berkeley, California, the Hyde Park area in Chicago and in New York's borough of Manhattan. But because it had little footing in the working class and minority neighborhoods where Democrats were strongest in general elections, its electoral fortunes were mixed. New York's New Democratic Coalition's initials (NDC) many old-timers suggested actually stood for "November Don't Count." It was, in a sense a bad rap: in Pat Brown's victory over Richard Nixon in California, Mario Cuomo's election as Governor of New York, and in numerous races for local office, the reformers were effective in forming alliances with regular organization Democrats in Black and Latino areas; but it remains a cautionary tale.

Such alliances can be formed and sustained. In Brooklyn, New York activists mobilized by Barak Obama's 2008 campaign approached the King's county Democratic organization about joining the county committee and were told, "Do not do this, do not run for county committee, just volunteer." Forming a New Kings movement, the activists found that they could not only win committee seats, but that in many cases– due to vacancies– all they had to do was file. There is still friction within the county organization, and the old-timers are still in charge, but the dynamic has changed.[10] The New Kings have morphed from pariahs to players. Gaining access to, or taking over a previously impermeable organization is a good thing to do; but significant battles to change the direction of American politics in 2020 need to extend far beyond Brooklyn. What are the alternatives– beyond clicking on a box in your e-mail to send a few dollars to distant candidate– for people who live in one of the roughly 350 House districts or twenty-odd states that are safe for one party or the other?

At least four percent of Americans own more than one home. Factor in students at residential colleges, and those who live in one place but frequently overnight in another, and there are as many as ten percent of us who legitimately can claim voting residence in more than one place. (Correction: you cannot vote in more than one place, that's a felony; but you can register in the one of your choice.) Check the politics and register in a place with more competitive races. Just as money flows across district lines so can voters and volunteers. And whether you change your voting place, having a local tie is an asset. It's both knowing the neighborhood and saying, "I live down the street and want to talk to you about the upcoming election," and "I want to talk to you about the election." The next best thing to having a second residence is having a relative in one: if you live in a Philadelphia district that is safely Democratic, but your daughter is in a more competitive area, you might go door-to-door there. The point is that personal contacts count, particularly when reinforced by an understandings of the district.

## Mapping the District

The average size of a congressional district, based on the 2010 census, was close to 650,000. It is now close to 740,000. Some, declining in population or heavy in non-citizens who count for apportionment but cannot vote, have fewer potential voters; others– particularly in rapidly growing suburbs– have far more and will wait until after the 2020 elections when the new census will serve to again make districts of equal size. At an average of 2.6 persons per household, nonetheless, each congressional district will have something like 270,000 households. Volunteers can only knock on so many of these doors, forcing campaigns to rely on polls, past election patterns and demographic statistics to target areas where volunteers, mailings and so on are likely to be most effective. Over time, in many areas it actually can be done. There were volunteers in some of the 2018 races described in chapter one who visited many hundreds of homes, sometimes visiting twice and making a follow-up get-out-the-vote call. At the other extreme, a number of people put in an afternoon or two, contacting perhaps fifty households. A little simple math suggests that it would take an army of at least 1800 door-to-door workers averaging 150 contacts each to saturate a congressional district. There are a number of ways, however, in which this task can become less formidable.

To begin, an effective campaign does not treat all citizens equally. When you pick cherries, as campaign consultant Matt Reese was fond of saying, you start where cherries grow. Political maps begin with data from past elections. The most useful, inexpensive and politically useful information one can have is a district's voting history. Given a finite source of volunteers the first place to look for progressive (or conservative) votes is in areas that have voted for progressive candidates in the past but have low or highly variable turnout rates, or for what are called "switch/split districts" where preferences may be variable. But this is only the starting point in an increasingly refined search for that subset of voters most likely to be receptive to the campaign's appeals. In some popular writing, campaigns have this down pat, and can know everything about individual voters except the color of their underwear. Eitan Hersh, calling this "the information fallacy," argues that, "When campaigns perceive voters, they do not see the opinions, traits, and behaviors that voters see in themselves. They see *perceived voters,* a simplified and distorted version of the electorate that is based on the data available to them."[11]

This has, in a sense, been the problem of every campaign, no matter how it is run. The traditional mapping of a district involved sifting through polls, past election returns and demographic variables to rather crudely locate clusters of believers. Working through existing groups from labor unions to rotary clubs and local businesses the goal was to connect campaign issues to various blocs of perceived voters. Virtually every campaign, to one degree or another, targets voters through these networks. Candidates' nights, unavoidable even if they seldom produce new supporters, and less formal events– at lunch breaks in factories, at regular meetings of clubs, at their fund-raising events– that provide opportunities to go one-on-one, meeting people on their own turf on the tacit assumption that the people at these places and events represent some larger group. And groups can, in a sense, be created. "Big Jim" Folsom, arguably Alabama's most progressive Governor, would drive into a small town, go to the general store to buy lunch or a cup of coffee and talk with the owner, then sit on the sidewalk to talk with anyone who came along. Those were simpler days, and even in rural areas walking into the Dollar Store is not the same as the general store of sixty years ago. Suburban areas with shifting populations, malls and supermarkets are more challenging; but local volunteers can almost always point candidates to a local establishment– a church, garden store or hair-dresser– that has the pulse of some segment of the community. It's an educational opportunity for the candidate, and while it may not earn many direct votes it helps establish a buzz.

Different today are the increasingly sophisticated shortcuts that simplify such efforts. For many years, campaigns could compile or purchase "prime" voter lists, particularly useful in low turnout or primary elections that identified– on the basis of past behavior– those most likely to vote. Such lists are becoming increasingly sophisticated indicating both who is likely to vote and how. Following the 2004 elections, Howard Dean, as Chairman of the Democratic National Committee, put together a team of sophisticated geeks who created VoteBuilder, a continuously up-dated data base housed in the DNC and available to state party organizations. It significantly, "extended the ability of the party and its candidates to contest elections," allowing "Democratic candidates for office from state senator to president to share data across campaigns and election cycles, while ensuring that the voter file was continuously updated with quality data.[12] Both parties now have this capacity, but the question of who should have access to this resource has yet to be resolved. In 2016 when some techy members of the Sander's campaign managed to hack Clinton's customized files, the DNC suspended Sander's use of VoteBuilder. The issue was resolved within twenty-four hours, but it highlighted what is an ongoing controversy.     Currently, the national committees control access to these files for presidential campaigns, carefully fire-walling each candidates' particular uses of the data. Fifty state parties control access for their own campaigns. Obviously, the chances are good that this results in a tilt toward incumbents, with some states even denying access to challengers. Even more controversial is the possibility that the efforts of the national committees and of the Senate and House campaign committees– which are growing increasingly active in candidate recruitment– will use access to these data bases to override the preferences of local groups. Daniel Kreiss, who has explored these issues as closely as anyone, argues that nothing precludes independent candidates from developing their own data bases, and that as long as the process of access is fair, these files are "a distinctively *partisan* resource," and should be valued as such. Generally, "it is a good thing that as a multi-issue coalition of heterogeneous actors the Democratic

Party sets its own policies and procedures for its use as a database."[13] That depends in turn on whether the folks in Washington (or Austin or Annapolis) can keep their thumbs off the scale. Logic suggests that if they want to win as many races as possible, the national parties will not override the clear preferences of local party activists, but logic and politics do not always coincide as the Democrats heavy-handed attempts to discourage insurgents in 2019-20 have shown.

Unconstrained by these issues, private companies are moving into the field and are– in many cases– more sophisticated than those of the party organizations. The data bases of companies like Catalist and Resonate provide a rich starting point for activists. The dream of national leaders "to create whole citizens in data," or "to use digital observational technologies and databases developed over the past two decades to reveal and leverage the psychological dispositions and social lives of citizens for electoral purposes"[14] is not yet a reality, and it is not certain that it should be. No matter how good the algorithms, they identify "perceived" voters, not real ones. Having people in place throughout a district, however, who are armed with data identifying hard core supporters, opponents and neutrals, is not unrealistic at all. Indeed it is how future campaigns can be both more effective and democratic, and how we can make politics up close and personal once again. Unlike electronic data bases running on their own, local groups using these files can help to actually repersonalize contacts between voters and elected politicians. Local activists, who can bridge the lines between individuals as whole people and their entries on a digital map, like the old precinct captains of the machine age, are the key to this kind of "new" politics. What the computer models misses is the interactive processes that made the old machines work: you canvas not just to sell your candidates or get out the vote, but to connect citizens to their polity. In the narrowest sense, the point of going door-to-door is to build a new data base or revise one found by the computers, register new voters and get your supporters to the polls. More importantly, it connects people with their government. The individual volunteer may not know about how to connect with social security, resolve a citizenship question, apply for a student or small business loan; but the point of organization is to link people with experts who can answer these questions. An effective political club can go beyond getting out the vote in a single election to developing both an actual and virtual map of the district.

Properly designed, well-coached canvassers can also flesh out the crude data from polls and feed information back to those who take subsequent surveys.

The argument for buying a system like Resonate is that allows canvassers (or advertisers) more accurately how to target their messages. Extreme negative contacts not only waste time but can discourage volunteers. (It is hard to knock on the next door having just been called a traitor, subjected to a racist screed, or physically threatened). Resonate provides what it calls "deep segmentation" to merge continuously updated survey data with demographics to provide clusters of perceived voters, giving door-to-door volunteers a reasonably accurate indicator of what to expect at each door. Their coverage is not only more extensive than those of the parties' but it provides refinements that go beyond a simple left-right continuum. Ideally, it can show volunteers not only what houses to avoid, but what kind of approach to each household is likely to prove most efficacious.

A good canvas provides more than information and mobilization. It also involves the development of a sense of these individuals as real people with political ideas, needs and issue concerns. Effective campaigning is in part about techniques, psychological dispositions, the targeting key groups and demographic analyses; but it also about representation and continuing dialogues between politicians and their constituents about public policy. In 1979, Richard Fenno argued that "the more fragmented and kinetic American society becomes, the more difficult it will be for House members to reach people."[15] Even then, no matter how he or she allocates time, it is possible to reach "a relatively few people directly." All of the candidates in Fenno's landmark study believed, however, "That as a result of their direct contact with as many supportive constituencies as they can reach, they will also reach a great many more people indirectly. They are great believers in the two-step flow of communications. They have to be. But they also think that it works."[16] As with Big Jim Folsom, it wasn't so much the people who sat with him on the sidewalk, but those who weren't there but heard that he had been. It is a form of advertising that is made effective by its interactive nature. The key to rebuilding the Democratic Party is to cumulate every one of these encounters into the data base, to develop a person by person map of every town, district and state that informs every ensuing campaign.

The best and most important way of perceiving the political dynamics of a neighborhood is to make canvassing a continuing process rather than a single-election event. In the Downtown Independent Democrats in the 1970s, we had an index card on every voter in our six election districts that were updated over a couple of evenings every year. They were annotated with a mixture of gossip ("Oh, Bill Smith, cross him off, they divorced, she got the loft and he's back in Kansas") issues ("very big on gay rights") and politics ("hates Ed Koch, loves Bella Abzug"). When each local volunteer went out door-to-door or on the phone, checking the cards against the new voter lists, he or she learned who the newly registered voters were and knew something about most of the rest. And this was a tough area to canvas. Unlike a rural district where the problem is the distance between houses, in the early days of Soho and Tribeca many of the loft dwellers were illegal and had no doorbells or intercoms. (To visit, you used a "Soho doorbell" shouting up from the street hoping someone would throw down the key to let you in). Reverse phone books helped identify some residents, looking for lighted rooms at night and ferns (or pot plants) in the widows, or just neighbors knowing neighbors helped build the list. But the key to success was the year in and year out persistence of the effort. As an added bonus, as the D.I.D. got to know its constituents they got to know us and to rely on our endorsements for less visible offices. Add computers instead of index cards, add the algorithms of Resonate or Catalyst, follow up canvassing with targeted e-mails and flyers, and the effectiveness of the post-modern campaign will both win elections and improve democracy.

Let's get real here. First of all, the computers are useful tools but do not provide solutions to all things political. Nor will you ever find enough volunteers for the kind of field operations needed to win. A lot of ardent, political people are simply uncomfortable going door-to-door or contacting strangers by phone. Not only do people lie, but political volunteers consistently over-estimate support by interpreting polite agreement as real accord. And in many of the areas where turnout is lowest, and where canvassing might do the most good, volunteers are scarce. The D.I.D., for all its data bases, was able to ally with like-minded groups in Chinatown, but never really establish a canvassing operation there. Economically marginal areas, where few people have the time or the interest in going door-to-door, are often those in which voter turnout is most problematic. Neighborhoods with large immigrant populations, both legal and eligible to vote and illegal and not eligible, are careful about opening the door to strangers. Yet these are the areas in which progressive candidates tend to do best, but where turnout is tricky. In the 2017 special congressional election in Georgia, the Democrat would almost certainly would have won if as many African-American voters turned out as had done so in 2016, or, even more decisively, as they did three years later in Stacy Abrams' campaign for Governor. There is no organizational challenge more important to the Democratic Party than that of broadening its volunteer and voter base in minority areas. It is ironic that the party most generally supportive of affirmative action in principle has given so little attention to it practice. One solution, not really that difficult, is to pay people to go door-to-door in their own neighborhoods. While it may raise distasteful memories of the old machines, part-time jobs registering voters and getting them to the polls, involving citizens who could not otherwise afford the time, and, coincidentally helping the campaign cannot be all bad.

Although language barriers pose a clear problem in some ethnic enclaves, experiments have shown that it is not at all clear that "canvassers who 'match' the ethnic profile of the neighborhood tend to have more success than those who do not."[17] There is, however, considerable evidence that those who have local ties are more effective than outsiders.[18] It would seem to follow that organizational sensitivity to neighborhood concerns is worth developing and, hopefully, sustained either by strengthening the formal party structure or creating a parallel system of clubs. In reform politics there is no substitute for organization. Absent the levers of patronage and pelf that sustained the old machines, the challenge today is that of sustaining the enthusiasm of volunteers. While defeat is often the mother of organization, success can help sustain political organizations by providing both hope and solid connections with those in power. Annual or twice-a-year reports from elected officials both help them keep in touch and increase interest in the club. In states with referenda, bringing in experts to explain their effects; meetings on college admissions, social security and local issues; purely social events, and the usual things that voluntary organizations do can help. In the heyday of New York City's Village Independent Democrats, there were people who looked forward more to the post-meeting beers at the Lion's Head than to the meetings themselves.

Two small caveats are in order here. The core purpose of a political organization is to win elections, not to hold fund-raisers and social events. Care must be taken not build political "aircraft carriers," organizations whose primary function becomes that of sustaining itself. A modern aircraft carrier has a base cost of roughly fourteen billion dollars. More than half of that cost is for a heavily armed hull– to protect the aircraft carrier; sophisticated radar systems– to protect the aircraft carrier; anti-aircraft and other arms– to protect the aircraft carrier; 20 or so fighter planes, in addition to those that perform the carrier's core missions– to protect the aircraft carrier. Once deployed, moreover, each carrier is accompanied by another fourteen billion dollars worth of other ships whose mission is . . . to protect the aircraft carrier. The withering of organizations begins when they similarly focus more on protecting themselves than they do on elections. All too often, party organizations spend more effort fending off primary challenges to their county and state committee members than they do in welcoming new members In state after state in 2016, Democratic organizations, instead of welcoming the energized supporters of Bernie Sanders, treated them as if they were enemies. Many Sander's supporters, in turn, responded by acting as if Hilary Clinton and the so-called party establishment was a greater enemy than Donald Trump.

A related problem with most organizations stems from what the German sociologist Roberto Michels called the "iron law of oligarchy." Disturbed that Europe's social democratic parties, despite their strong support for democracy, were in their own internal governance all but immune to internal challenges, Michels suggested that parties and other membership organizations were almost invariably doomed to oligarchy. Once a leadership team is in place, efficiency demands the kind of specialized division of labor found in bureaucracies; and as organizations becomes bureuacratized the gap between the skills of leaders and the rank and file becomes virtually unbreachable. To be successful, parties need professionals on top. Once on top, those same professionals control the mailing lists, the meeting agendas, and files that give them virtual immunity to challenge.[19] This same dynamic, as it increasingly alienates the rank and file, may in the long run contain the seeds of its own destruction. This, in a way, was the fate of Tammany: the more tightly its leadership resisted internal dissent, the more the pressures for change expanded until they exploded into formal challenges. Bureaucratic parties similarly run the risk of simply fading away. Long out of touch with changing electorates, they become so remote that they no longer know how to win, and like Congressman Crowley in 2018, they lose. The best cure for this kind of problem begins with awareness and goes to bringing in new members, recruiting new leaders and avoid putting too much responsibility in the hands of too few people.

The modern campaign replaced the old ward healers with professionals. "The modern campaign, often called a candidate-centered operation, might actually be 'consultant-centered.'"[20] Using sophisticated polls to identify major issues and constituencies, the goal was "message consistency," in which various media would be to put forth "a variety of messages" all related "to a single core theme."[21] The post-modern campaign, with micro-targeting can expand this variety of messages, direct them to specific voters, and receive running data in return. It can bring together volunteers and voters who share a primary concern with, say, environmental issues, target social media and mailing to such subgroups, and feed their reactions back to the campaign.

## What About Issues?

The basic strategy of a people-to-people campaign is not much different from a traditional media campaign in its inherent conservatism. It seeks less to prostelitize than to mobilize voters as they are, in terms of their own issue priorities and beliefs. As a matter of efficiency it begins with the activation of the party's existing base– picking cherries where the cherries are– before reaching out. One close student of realigning elections argues that, "Although it may be tactically effective, the base strategy is also dangerous because it actively discourages desperately needed innovation and ideas."[22] Even with the feedback loops that canvassing can provide, the post-modern campaign takes voters and issues pretty much as they are. Except insofar as Donald Trump's nationalist agenda may be reshaping the ways in which some sectors of the electorate view the parties,

> America's two major parties continue on like automatons making the same old arguments over the same old issues as if by rote, while in reality there is little to debate. . . . The New Deal debate is over and most of what remains is just the kabuki theater of campaigns, politics for the sake of politics, symbolism, and spoils. We've reached the long empty part

of a party system in which an era's great debate is done but
the next one has yet to arrive.[23]

As some of the poll data cited in this chapter show, the economic driver
of the old New Deal coalition no longer explains what issues most divided
Americans today. Yet, as DiStefano argues, candidates of both parties
continue to focus their campaigns on these issues. Even the self-described
"progressive" Democrats and "nationalist" Republicans say relatively little on
the campaign trail about issues other than the top two or three in the polls,
and in both cases, they tend to fall back into the well-worn contours of the
past. Instead of a European-style socialist health system what progressive
Democrats are promoting is continuation of the free enterprise, insurance
based system of fee-for-service medicine based on the Social Security and
Medicaid models debated for more than half a century. Their environmental
proposals, as indicated by the green "New Deal" title are essentially those
of the traditional subsidy and economic models of most recent Democratic
campaigns. And although the President and a handful of Republican
legislators frequently play the nationalist card, their message increasingly
circles back to the traditional Republican trio of deregulation, tax cuts and
opposition to "socialism." If there is a realignment that changes these lines of
conflict, it is more likely to emerge from conversations in the field than from
candidates and their campaigns. Putting people back in politics insofar as
it lets a thousand flowers bloom in terms of issues, may be the best available
vehicle for doing this.

The prospects for real change on most of these issues depend for their
prospects on first dealing with the meta-issues of system reform. No President
has used and abused executive orders more in shaping public policy than
Donald Trump. Obama too (and Bush before him) used these putative
powers to excess, though not as blatantly. Much of this authority derives
increasingly from both explicit delegations of power from the Congress and
a monumental failure on the part of the legislative branch to enact real laws.
Not only is the White House empowered increasingly to "fill in the details"
of increasingly vague acts of Congress, but private interests too are granted
the authority to, in effect, govern themselves. Public policy remains, even
more than when Lowi argued, half a century ago, is less about the rule of
law than the summing of private deals, politics at the expense of policy.[24]

# Endnotes

1   David S. Broder, The Party's Over: The Failure of Politics in America (New York: Harper and Row, 1971).

2   Alex Fouinaies and Andrew B. Hall, "How Divisive Primaries Hurt Parties: Evidence from Near-Runoffs (May 4, 2016). Available at SSRN: http://ssrn.com/abstract=27755324.

3   Stephen L. Morgan and Jiwon Lee, "Trump Voters and the White Working Class," 4 Sociological Science (November 2017), 687.

4   John H. Aldrich, James L. Carson, Brad T. Gomez and David W. Rohde, Change and Continuity in the 2016 and 2018 Elections (Washington: CQ Press, 2019), 23.

5   Alan I. Abromowitz,"The Trump Effect: The 2018 Election on a Polarizing President," in Larry Sabato and Kyle Kondik, eds., The Blue Wave: The 2018 Midterms and What They Mean for the 2020 Elections (Lanham, MD: Rowman and Littlefield, 2019), 43.

6   E. E. Schattschneider, The SemiSovereign People: A Realists View of Democracy in America (New York: Holt, Rinehart and Winston, 1960), 63.

7   Abramowitz, 26.

8   Jamelle Bouie, "The Senate Is as Much of a Problem as Trump, The New York Times, (May 12, 2019), Sunday Review, 4.

9   William Riordan, Plunkitt of Tammany Hall (New York: Dutton, 1963)). 51.

10   Danielle Tcholakian, "Challenging the Party Establishment," The New York Times, September 3, 2017, WE7.

11   Eitan D. Hersh, Hacking the Electorate: How Campaigns Perceive Voters (New York: Cambridge Univeristy Press, 2015). 12.

12   Daniel Kreiss, Taking Our Country Back: The Crafting of Network Politics From Howard Dean to Barak Obama (New York: Oxford University Press, 2012), 16.

13   Daniel Kreiss, Prototype Politics: Technology-Intensive Campaigning and the Data of Democracy (New York: Oxford University Press, 2016), 212-13.

14   Ibid., 215.

15   Richard F. Fenno, Jr, Home Style: House Members in Their Districts (Boston: Little, Brown and Company, 1978), 236.

16   Ibid., 237.

17   Donald P. Green and Alan S. Gerber, Get Out the Vote: How to Increase Voter Turnout (Washington: Brookings Institution Press, 2015), 33.

18   Ibid.

19   Roberto Michels, Political Parties: A Sociological Study of the Oligarchical Tendencies of Modern Democracy (Origially published in Germany in 1916 and available in English in a number of formats and editions).

20 Daniel M. Shea and Michael John Burton, Campaign Craft: The Strategies, Tactics, and Art of Political Campaign Management (Westport, CT: Praerger, 3rd ed., 2006), 12.

21 Ibid., 23.

22 Frank J. DiStefano, The Next Realignment: Why America's Parties are Crumbling and What Happens Next (Amherst, NY: Prometheus Books, 2019), 343.

23 Ibid., 258.

24 Theodore J. Lowi, The End of Liberalism: The Second Republic of the United States (New York: W.W. Norton and Co., 1969).

## Chapter 3

# Campaign Strategies and Tactics

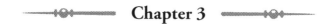
*Executive Summary and Action Agenda*

Capturing the process of finding candidates who can win in November is one of the first priorities of citizen activists. As a first step this means developing organizations that transcend the official town and county lines that define party organizations. Realistically, at most a quarter of all legislative seats in Congress and at the state level are competitive; but looking forward to reapportionment in 2021, the game becomes considerably more open and complex. The first priority in 2020 is to target seats that have been closely contested in past. The shifting of party dynamics moving through 2020 that might begin to tip the balance and impact the calculus of redistricting in 2021 suggest that although few districts are totally beyond redemption, the key to realistic change will be found in these generally marginal states and areas.

In the last presidential election (2016) an average of about 280,000 citizens voted in each congressional district. In districts where there were competitive primaries in both major parties voter turnout was never more than 80,000. Here is where local party activists and other volunteers– if they can coordinate with each other– can have a highly disproportionate impact on the system. Their work should begin long before the actual primary, seeking first to find a candidate who can win in November and second to prevent the kind of divisive primary that might make victory more difficult.

Capturing the process of finding candidates who can win in November is one of the first priorities of citizen activists. As a first step this means developing organizations that transcend the official town and county lines that define party organizations. Realistically, at most a quarter of all legislative seats in Congress and at the state level are competitive; but looking forward to reapportionment in 2021, the game becomes considerably more open and complex. The first priority in 2020 is to target seats that have been closely contested in past. The shifting of party dynamics moving through 2020 that might begin to tip the balance and impact the calculus of redistricting in 2021 suggest that although few districts are totally beyond redemption, the key to realistic change will be found in these generally marginal states and areas.

It is important to recognize at the outset that a balanced ticket is probably a good thing, and that unions, ethnic organizations and other organized groups cannot be dismissed out of hand because they are not with you on every issue. Once organized, the first job of any grassroots campaign is to help and persuade some of the one third of those eligible to vote that they should register. With mail-in registration in all fifty states, there are still many potential voters who find the process difficult. This is low-hanging fruit, and there is nothing more effective that volunteers can do toward winning elections than registering new voters.

Once the candidate has won the nomination or a clear path to it, he or she will have access to the increasingly sophisticated data bases of the state and national parties, but nothing is better than door-to-door work in compiling lists of real as opposed to virtual voters. There must be enough local input to be sure that the campaign message is crafted in terms of local concerns and the nature of the opposition. Next in effectiveness to a registration drive is getting out the vote on the basis of individual contacts with voters. A good canvas that identifies supporters, converts a few, supplies absentee ballot applications, helps with early voting, and reminds supporters to vote on election day generally adds as many as fifty votes per precinct. Direct mobilization has been shown to have a greater effect than all other forms of candidate spending. Putting people back in politics works.

Action Points:

- Organization is essential, either work with the existing party structure, take it over, or organize a parallel system of clubs.

- For most offices in most parts of the country, primary elections, those in which the parties nominate their candidates, as important and easier to influence than the November general elections.

- The single most important criteria in backing primary candidates is whether they can win in November. The best indicators are that they have strong local ties, the ability to raise money, and have won other offices.

- A registration drive is the first step in mapping the district, identifying supporters and recruiting other volunteers. Properly done, it is far more effective than converting those already registered.

- Good politics is a function of good lists. The best lists come from neighbors working their neighborhoods.

- Having identified your supporters, it takes an Election Day operation to get their actual votes.

## What Works and What Doesn't

Issues, candidates and ideologies aside, most campaigns look pretty much alike. You don't see yard signs in the downtown areas of large cities or window signs in the country, yet you could walk into the headquarters of any campaign in the country– north, south, east, west; Republican, Democrat; incumbent or challenger– and see the same basic activities. And surprisingly little has changed over time. E-mail has made the old job of "lick 'em and stick 'em" less formidable with laptops replacing piles of brochures on every improvised desk. Torchlight parades are rare. Most states now outlaw the free beer nights that breweries would throw for their favored candidates. There are no smoke-filled rooms. But the people in those now airier rooms are doing pretty much what they did fifty years ago. Some are designing and distributing leaflets, organizing walk lists and mobilizing volunteers or paid workers; media people are preparing press releases and daily blasts as they simultaneously monitor the coverage they are getting. The candidate– if he or she is in the headquarters– is almost certainly on the phone raising money. There are volunteers compiling and refining lists of voters. Someone is working on signs. An in-house pollster or hired company is coordinating with the campaign manager. A volunteer or hired hand is doing opposition research and tracking its campaign. Early in the campaign there are people working on voter registration. At least one person is scheduling the candidate's appearances, finding surrogates where needed, and coordinating with other candidates and office holders. The list goes on.

Despite growing professionalization, what is perhaps most fascinating about these activities is how little their cost-effectiveness or general efficacy has been really studied. The day after the election, as the loser's supporters gather to collect their effects and say their goodbyes, they seldom ask whether having the paper coffee cups emblazoned with the candidates' name won any votes, or whether the get-out-the-vote flyers they hung on every door actually helped.

> The paper trail that might illuminate what actually happened– the binders filled with polling data, the hard drives filled with data bases accounting for every direct contact made with a voter– usually end up in the nearest Dumpster. Often no one even convenes a postmortem among the staff operatives, consultants and candidate to talk about what went wrong and why.[1]

There are good reasons that campaigns seldom seriously examine questions of what works and what does not. Any decent test of various techniques requires measuring its use with one sample of the population against a control group that was not exposed to the technique. But the very idea of a control group, or as the campaign manager would put it, a group whose votes we don't go after, is anathema to a serious candidate. Thus, "While much has been written on how parties raise money, relatively little has been offered on how that money is spent."[2] There are, at the same time, enough historical campaigns in similar areas with different campaign priorities that a rough outline of what works best under what conditions is emerging. Let's look at the evidence through the major stages of a campaign.

## Candidates

A handful of candidates are more coroneted than elected. In the days of machine politics, it was possible for an unknown party loyalist to use the organization's control of the process to win local or state office and perhaps a seat in congress. Complete unknowns can still win local offices simply because no one else wants to run. By-and-large, however, people have to know who you are. In most states today party organizations influence but seldom control nominations, which means that celebrities, those who already hold elective office and people with money are particularly advantaged whether or not they make the best candidates. And here is where citizen activists can play the absolutely vital roles of recruiting, sorting, and endorsing the candidates who have both political integrity and the best chances of winning. When you join a club, attend a caucus, volunteer or vote in a primary, you are a recruiter.

In the wake of the still-contentious 2016 Democratic primaries, there will almost certainly be sharp intra-party divisions in 2020 that will trickle down to lower layers of the ticket. As we argued in chapter 2, divisive primaries, unless they are highly polarized do not necessarily hurt candidates in the general election; but they do waste resources and can leave enduring scars. The first and foremost priority of the old machines was to avoid such dissension through control of the nominating process. The old progression of candidacy from party to local office, perhaps a foray into state politics, then Congress has been displaced by the lateral entry of individuals who jump this progression by virtue of fame in another area or, more commonly, by having a lot of money. Also more common is the recruitment of candidates by ideologically motivated outside groups financing primary campaigns as a way to warn incumbents that they will face similar challenges. In many races, however, the problem is less one of candidates jumping into the fray than of finding a qualified person to give up her chosen occupation, disrupt his personal life, and open herself to public criticism and the possibility of humiliating defeat. Realistically, candidate recruitment begins with the proposition– in a country where fewer than half of its citizens engage in so minimal a political act as voting– that few qualified candidates will be found. More than forty percent of all state legislative seats and as many as twenty percent in the House of Representatives are typically uncontested by one of the major parties.

In Chicago's Daley organization, as in all the old machines, candidate recruitment was part of an overall process of constructing a slate. Assembling a ticket involved "taking into consideration the interests of the various groups which make up the local Democratic Party."[3] While loyalty to the organization was important, the primary consideration was to pick candidates who could win. It was, as Milton Rakove describes it, "an exercise in science and art– in the science of constructing a well-balanced ticket and the art of pacifying the various groups that make up the electorate."[4] The decline of party machines and the controlling influence of primary elections has made it all but impossible to cover all the bases, but the principle of picking candidates primarily on their basis of their ability to win in November is still paramount. Add up all the pros and cons, in these partisan days, and the chances are that the worst Democrat running in your district will be better on 95 out of hundred issues than his or her November opponent. If you put all of the issues on a one-to-ten, left-right scale, as one of my friends put it during the Democratic presidential primaries, if Elizabeth Warren is a two-to-three, and Joe Biden or four or five, the most moderate Republican is an eight or nine. For more than a decade now, not a single Democrat in the House has had a more conservative voting record than the most liberal Republican.[5] The ways in which progressive Democrats, moreover, become committee chairs (as opposed to ranking minority members) is by having Democratic majorities in the House and Senate.

Successful recruitment efforts are founded in previous organizational work. In persuading someone to run, the old machines could promise the support of a tested campaign organization, financial support and immediate access to a roster of campaign professionals. The greater the extent to which a popular movement can assemble such resources, the more likely it is to find capable, electable candidates. A little more than ten years ago, a group of people in my upstate New York congressional district, working largely over the internet, put together a "true blue" network of Democrats working to end Republican domination of the district. With no particular candidate in mind, they established a network of like-minded voters spanning a half dozen counties, created a roster of volunteers and secured financial pledges. By the time Kirsten Gillibrand decided to run, much of the preliminary work of organizing a campaign was done, and she won in a closely contested race. Redistricting, after the 2010 census, split the district and the organization more or less faded away, but there are signs of revival that are very important to both immediate and long term success. Again, political influence is a process not an event.

Surveys have shown that voters have rather consistently sought certain personal characteristics in candidates. The most important is experience, closely followed in most surveys by honesty, intelligence and education.[6] In my own fifty years spending time on Capitol Hill, it is striking how much slimmer and better kept members of Congress have become, enough to suggest that the media have made looks an issue. Fewer and fewer members of Congress are veterans of the military, but it still appears to be of positive value, as it is to be neither "too young" nor "too old." Some prejudices are still found (and probably under-reported) particularly against women and certain ethnic groups and religions. These predilections and prejudices are eroding and can be overcome in most districts if confronted head on. "Put a lantern on it," as John F. Kennedy did in raising the question of his Roman Catholic faith at the outset of his 1960 campaign for president, preempting those who could give it a less favorable spin. In many cases, moreover, being a member of a minority can politically overcome prejudice through the pride of fellow group members. Just as there were voters who opposed Obama on racial grounds, their votes seem to have been offset by record turnout in African-American communities.

As important as these attributes might be, certain more controllable factors count for more. The first, most and increasingly most important of these is having lots of money and/or access to it. For the first time in history, a majority of those elected to the house in 2016 were millionaires. Rich people are doubly advantaged: they both have money of their own and they know lots other people who do. Thanks to the Supreme Court, it is not just rich people we are talking about, but *very rich* people. The 2010 ruling in *Citizens United v. Federal Elections Commission,* in which the Court held that groups independent of actual campaign committees could make unlimited donations to independent political groups; and the less publicized 2014 decision in *McCutcheon v. FEC,* which ruled that ceilings on the aggregate amounts that individuals could give to political action committees, parties and so on were also illegal, changed the rules of the game. By elevating the phrase "money talks" from irony to constitutional doctrine, the Court dramatically changed the political landscape. The best-financed campaigns do not always win, frequently they just find ways to waste more money. Campaign consultants will tell you, on the other hand, that money can buy campaign workers but volunteers do not pay for media time or utility bills. True enough, but what they can do is to raise enough money to be viable, to use free media, to provide rent-free spaces for events, and to reach voters more effectively through neighbor-to-neighbor appeals. And there remain some restrictions on money in politics that give volunteer campaigns at a comparative advantage. The only ways in which big bucks can (legally) flow to individual campaigns is either through party committees or independent political action committees that cannot coordinate their expenditures with actual candidates. In contrast with the nimble ability of a local volunteer campaign to taylor its message to changing issues, campaigns whose funding comes largely from outside have relatively little control over the timing and substance of their own messages.

For candidates, local ties are important. While national celebrities like Robert Kennedy, Hilary Clinton and Mitt Romney can parachute into a state and win, it is difficult– absent strong family ties– for outsiders to attract either the volunteer base or the marginal voters needed to win. Although only about half the members of the current Senate were born in the states they now represent, only a handful lack significant local roots. And that percentage is even higher for the House. A successful candidate should have some base of community support. Even in the ethnic-charged atmosphere of Daley's Chicago, to use Rakove's example, "A Pole who has been active in the Polish National Alliance. . . would have much more attraction to slate makers than would a Polish lawyer who has had no interest in or concern with Polish affairs"[7]. Much more difficult to evaluate are questions of personality and morals. Divorce no longer seems to be a major factor, but accusations of sexual harassment increasingly are.

What may be most disturbing is the erosion in importance of the old-fashioned values of honesty and integrity. The Trumpian world of alternative truths, and his blatant violation of long accepted norms of openness, may have changed the political landscape for years to come. While I doubt that the values of corruption, collusion and nepotism have become anything like a new norm, it may no longer be important for candidates to reveal their personal financial holdings, give up financial holdings that conflict with their political roles, or separate family businesses from their political lives. Trump very cleverly hung a lantern on his conflicts of interest by blatantly making a virtue of his ability and resolve (later rescinded) to fund his own campaign. The notion that all politicians are corrupt has led many people, as Naomi Klein puts it, "to treat electoral politics as macabre entertainment. Once politics has reached such a debased state, why bother protecting it from a boor like Trump? It's a cesspool anyway, so let the game begin."[8]

Paradoxically, however, Trump's campaign itself may have shown that some old values still have legs. Citing her more than $20 million in speaking fees, the Clinton Foundation, and super-priced campaign fund-raising events, Trump's "crooked Hillary" theme eclipsed his own conflicts of interest in the 2016 polls. Clinton has never faced any legal challenges, but she, and other politicians, have had their images degraded by their fund-raising activities and connections with the rich and famous. Whether this is a cautionary tale for aspiring politicians is not clear, it may be more about spin than reality; what is clear is that the essential paradigm is changing.

There is by no means a large reservoir people dying to give up their day jobs to go into politics. I once had a student who was dating a woman whose father had agreed to run a token campaign in a district that had almost never voted for a Democrat. Having started a successful business, he thought it would be a good way to get to know his neighbors and help other Democrats running for local office. My student was with the family as the returns come in showing a Democratic landslide. When it was announced that the businessman had won he burst into tears: "I don't want to be in Congress. I hate Washington," he cried, "What the hell am I going to do?" (P. S. He served four terms.) If winning is upsetting to some, losing is not fun either. Especially in seats not rated competitive, it can be difficult to find a warm body for even a token campaign. Possible candidates can be found among newer lawyers, accountants and real estate agents who can use the publicity as a sort of legitimate advertising. Academics have the summer to mount credible campaigns, as can retirees who may enjoy the challenge. What is crucial in persuading such people is the existence of a group of volunteers ready and willing to work and enough pledges and promises of funding to mount at least a respectable campaign.

There are no rewards in politics for finishing second, but it is not trivial to have someone on the ballot to help the rest of the ticket and if only because major upsets do occur. Eric Cantor, who many thought to be in line for the speakership, lost to an unknown in a 2014 primary largely because his Washington work had led him to ignore his district, much as Democratic Majority Leader Tom Daschle lost his seat to Republican John Thune a decade before. And then there was Joe Crowley's infamous defeat in 2018. Indictments, deaths, unexpected retirements– stuff happens. More importantly, the seeming invulnerability of some incumbents, especially in changing districts, may be grounded less in their strengths than the weaknesses of previous challengers. Without gainsaying the difficulty of having an impact in a district "safe" for one party or the other, there is no such thing as a sure thing. One strong campaign that moves a district from 35% to 42 or 43 may attract more volunteers, more money and perhaps a stronger candidate two years later. The shifting of a district's partisan dynamic between 2018 and 2020 will also– for better or worse– be an important part of the calculus of redistricting in 2021. A strong case can be made for running twice, the first time to build an organization and gain name recognition, two years later to win. Six Democrats who had run unsuccessfully in 2016 increased their percentage of the vote by an average of 13.2 in 2018, with four of them winning.

## Organization

The period between when candidates announce their intentions and the state's filing deadlines occur, is when the role of citizen volunteers is at its maximum. If the party primary is the actual moment that counts, the winnowing period that precedes it gives an often decisive role to what we might call the "selectorate." Congressional districts vary increasingly in population the further in time from the last census to anywhere from half a million or so (for Alaska's one seat) to more than a million, and an average of roughly 710,000, 260,000 of whom voted in 2018.[9] In districts where there were competitive primaries the turnout for either party was never more than 80,000 and was often as little as fifteen percent of eligible voters.

> While the entire American nomination system is vulnerable to capture by factions within a political party, congressional primaries, especially for the House of Representatives, are particularly vulnerable, inexpensive, targets of opportunity for national ideological groups because they operate, in most years, in near total obscurity. With the exception of elections for local school boards, congressional primaries are among the most low turnout elections in the United States. They, therefore, provide the perfect setting for interest groups within a political party to gain and exercise influence out of proportion to their size.[10]

Here is where local party activists and other volunteers– if they can coordinate with each other– can have a disproportionate impact. Their work should begin long before the actual primary, seeking first to find a candidate who can win in November, second to prevent a divisive primary that might make victory more difficult, and only third to perform an ideological litmus test. This last point, which I've argued in previous chapters, is worth reiterating. Strong party discipline, particularly in the House, combined with growing polarization, has rendered the ideologies of individual members of Congress increasingly irrelevant. Even the handful of successful third party candidates– Bernie Sanders among them– join a major party caucus and follow their lead on most votes: they must if they want to get anything done. But more importantly, congressional parties have become so polarized in recent years the most conservative Democrat is more liberal than the most liberal Republican. The defeat of any Republican by any Democrat, in other words, moves the Congress to the left. If you want to move the Congress to the left, you must choose Democratic candidates less on the basis of their ideological purity than on their ability to win. A handful of more radical members can raise new issues and alter political dialogue, but they cannot substantially move public policy without more mainstream allies.

The more candidates there are in race, the more intense the need for vetting and working with the party structure and key groups in the district.

Looking back from November, there is hardly a candidate who would not agree that their campaign began too late. When the party's selectorate is unified, the primary election becomes the first round of working the district for November. This may not be easy but it remains important. And, of course, when the prospects of victory appear slim, few viable candidates will emerge absent a strong organizational base. It is never too early to begin both fund-raising and friend-raising, if only to make it easier for strong candidates to run. There are also more subtle reasons for developing strong local organizations. Only when the folks back home are a representative's primary support group can he or she have the independence to act as an ideological free agent in the Congress. Conversely, absent a strong local base, the more a candidate must turn to national organizations, wealthy political action committees and others who will gladly pay the pipers who later play their tunes.

The primary building blocks of viable organizations are such legally defined areas as towns and villages, counties, city council districts, assembly districts and so on. As argued in Chapter 2, most congressional districts overlap many such jurisdictions. Once the party's nominee is chosen, it is one of his or her major challenges to bring all these diverse constituencies together. In ten states, there are fewer than ninety days between the primary and general elections in which this can be done. The more local groups have already begun this process, the more effective the campaign. Unlike the districts for most state legislators, city councils, and municipalities which often have legally mandated party organizations, congressional district organizations must be voluntarily created. Whether this is done by official party leaders from a variety of the legally-mandated districts, by informal citizen groups, or a combination of both, it is an important step toward victory.

A major political problem is that of defining its relations with other organizations. The members and supporters of various progressive single-interest groups may be only peripherally interested in the campaign or even see it is a rival for funding and membership. It is a major task, as Michael Waltzer once put it, "to get people into the same bed who never imagined they could take a peaceful walk together."[11] Having the support of an interest group begins with the recognition that you are not going to win their support by pointing to your stands on other issues, and, on the part of the group, that while you might not give them all that they want, the alternative is worse. It behooves any successful campaign to reach out to sympathetic groups from the outset, to bring their leaders in, if possible, under the campaign tent. Absolute candor is vital here– you are dealing with people who know their stuff– and if your differences are real but marginal they may want to keep their support quiet; but ties with special interests are not only avenues to voters but access to information: who can better tell about problems with military hospitals than members of veterans groups? Some advocates of high tech campaigns argue that intermediary groups have lost their importance as candidates develop their own issue-segmented data bases. This both ignores the fact that these groups themselves can provide significant inputs to those algorithms but provide direct contacts to trusted voters themselves.

These contacts can also be useful in other ways. A group like lawyers, gays, or professors for Jones might bring people out who would not come to a less-specialized fund-raiser. Special groups such as these also provide a way of dispersing titles among supporters. The most important, and sometimes most difficult of these problems are in dealing with other campaigns. Congressional candidates must, of course, worry about Trump, the Democratic nominee and– in some states, the candidates for U. S. Senate; but they also have to worry about state senators and sheriffs, local officials and party regulars. Even so simple an issue as whether to have single candidate yard signs or those promoting the entire slate can be surprisingly troublesome. There just aren't any good rules, as you work in a campaign or try to build an organization, in which the existing party leaders and your campaign don't see eye to eye, or where your pro-choice candidate for Congress is on the same ticket as an anti-abortion State Senator. All things considered, a balanced ticket is probably an asset if only because each of its component candidates can increase turnout for the entire ticket. If you are running a campaign filled with volunteers and a newly active club, working with the regular party organization can pose problems. Precinct captains who have held their "jobs" for years may resent volunteers intruding on their turf, even if they themselves have not done squat for years. They may have cohorts of relatives and friends who turn out in sufficient numbers to keep them winning, but that doesn't mean they are still working. At the height of the club movement's power in the fifties and sixties, James Q. Wilson very perceptively described the tensions that often arose between amateur Democrats oriented toward particular candidates and issues, and the regular organization types whose interests were more toward organizational maintenance.[12] In post-modern politics, the hope is to fuse the two.

## Voter Registration

Discounting felons and those ineligible to vote for other legal reasons— such as severe mental illness or failure to establish residence— more than one citizen in four chooses not to become eligible to vote.[13] Race is much less a major factor in non-registration than it was fifty years ago, though this may be changing as growing number of states have recently passed voter identification laws that have discriminatory effects. Poverty and low education rates are generally the demographic variables most closely linked to low registration rates, as are certain ethnic factors. Forty-four percent of self-identified Asians and 46% Hispanics are not registered.[14] Registration also rather dramatically increases with age: less than half of 18-24 year olds were registered in 2018 as compared with nearly 73 per cent of citizens over 65.

Part of the problem is that in many states registering to vote is a more complicated process than that of actually casting a ballot. And there is growing evidence that persons with disabilities, visual problems in particular, face particular barriers in all but a handful of states.[15] Among the tens of millions of unregistered voters are some who refuse on principle— Don't Vote, It Only Encourages the Bastards— as a popular bumper sticker reads. For most, as the economist Anthony Downs once wrote, "every rational man decides to vote just as he makes all other decisions: if the returns outweigh the costs, he votes, if not, he abstains."[16] For candidates and their supporters, any effort that helps to decrease the perceived "costs" of registration, or increase the benefits is to mine an enormous, generally untapped mother lode of potential votes. In the 2016 presidential election, more than thirty million more citizens stayed home rather than vote for either Trump or Clinton. Today, more than ever, it is easier to bring some of these people into the system than to induce old partisans to change sides.

How can this be done? Most importantly and obviously, we can lower the costs of voting by bringing the opportunity directly to the unregistered. Under the Motor Voter law all fifty states must allow mail-in registration.

Ten states also allow full registration by e-mail, while another three offer limited access on line. Even then, the task can be confusing, and costly in terms of time. With volunteer help at the door, these costs can be virtually erased. Carrying application forms or mobile Wi-Fi units, volunteers can guide citizens through the registration process in a matter of minutes To the extent that citizens actually perform some sort of cost-benefit analysis in deciding whether to vote, we emphasize the cost side because the perceived benefit side of the equation is much more difficult to control. A primary determinant of voter turnout, as one recent study puts it, is "the level of uncertainty in the national campaign contest."[17] The more uncertain the outcome, in other words, or the greater the perceived differences between the candidates, the more people will see it in their interest to vote. Many state election calendars, unfortunately, require potential voters to register before most campaigns heat up. Registration drives in these areas must either be forward looking, or designed to sign people up after a divisive national election or controversial event.

The point is to register Democrats. As small "d" democrats, it would be unseemly to turn down others; but the point of a partisan registration drive is to target individuals with a high potential of being Democrats. Once again it's a matter of picking cherries where the cherries are. We will discuss targeting anon, but the point here is that there is nothing that volunteers can do that is more effective toward winning elections than registering new voters. And it can be done any time– years, and months ahead, and, in some states, right up until Election Day.

Would be that the issue were that simple. For many nonvoters the "costs" of voting go beyond time and confusion. There are voters, and this is a very tricky issue to poll, whose general suspicion of anything to do with the government leads them to believe that registering to vote will subject them to new taxes or other penalties. One survey found that twenty per cent of adults who had never voted expected their ballot to be marked for later examination, another twenty-five percent thought they would have to declare out loud who they were voting for.[18] Many others see little connection between voting and public policy. At the same time, a recent study by the Pew Research Center shows "that the unregistered population is not entirely unengaged from civic life."[19] Indeed, the study found that, "more than 40 percent of the unregistered cared who would win the presidency in 2016, and some indicated that they could be motivated to register in the future." These findings suggest that opportunities exist to bring large numbers of new voters into the system, if only by actually engaging them. As Murphy and I wrote in 1974:

> The key to voter registration is often social pressure. People vote because they are embarrassed not to, because their neighbors do, because it is accepted as one of the duties of a loyal American, or simply because someone asks them to. One reason that upper- and middle-income citizens are more likely to vote than the poor is that social pressures encouraging voting are much stronger in more affluent communities.[20]

Partly because voter registration has long been treated as a non-partisan civic exercise, most registration drives have been conducted by non-profits not parties. The parties' increasingly sophisticated ability to micro-target demographic groups, however, provides a growing ability to target and register only those most likely to support particular candidates. A "birthday program," for example, targeting African Americans when they turned eighteen, added thousands of Obama voters to the rolls in 2012. Once particular area have been targeted, direct mail appeals can have some effect, but the social pressure implicit in personal visits, with its combined power to explain the secret ballot and the process of registration is far more effective. After volunteers selectively canvas their own neighborhoods, the first step is to prioritize areas of Democratic strength, sending volunteers to them, and using phone and mail appeals to those further down on the list. In areas of high home ownership, voter files can be compared with property tax reports to show which households do not have registered voters. Sometimes electric company lists and city directories can be used to locate potential voters. The better one knows the neighborhood, the more common sense kicks in: if there are two registered voter in a house and three cars there is a good chance of finding an unregistered teenager. A fading bumper sticker for Trump is not a good sign.

It is best, particularly in neighborhoods not known to the volunteer, to have volunteers travel in pairs, preferably male and female, and to deploy at least one bi-lingual person in districts with known ethnic minorities. Most importantly, each campaign should provide a briefing sheet that explains local election laws in some detail, and a handout to remind residents of important dates and a phone number or e-mail address to contact if they have any problems. In most states, shopping malls and some private communities are allowed to deny access to political canvassers (though the legality of such bans has not been uniformly upheld). Keep it simple, with non-voters especially likely to confound slick with sleazy, a simple black and white printout will suffice at this stage. Before sending volunteers into a neighborhood, the campaign should first contact the local party organization and groups like labor unions that may already have targeted the same neighborhoods. Scripts can be found in any one of a dozen campaign manuals, and many volunteers will ask for one; but a neighborly conversational approach probably works best. Typically, a registration drive marks the beginning of a formal campaign, and it should be seen as an entry level platform for an increasingly refined process of voter identification. Its purpose is not simply to put new voters on the rolls but to serve as the first cut in the process of mapping the district and of getting voters to think about the upcoming election. And it is also an opportunity to find new recruits.

It is never too early to recruit volunteers—others to go door-to-door—and for those uncomfortable doing that, to answer the phones, prepare mailings, and so on. I've never known of a campaign that had too many volunteers, yet it is surprising how many recruitment opportunities are lost. Every time the candidate meets a potential volunteer, or someone offers to help there should be an immediate follow-up. Some campaigns go so far as to always have a supply of mailing lists and envelopes on hand just to keep people involved.

Perhaps the most fruitful orchards for picking cherries are those particularly targeted by an increasingly anti-immigrant Republican Party. Hispanics are, of course, the largest such group, but in the past ten years, in the borough of Queens, New York with carefully crafted Chinese and Korean language phone drives, the largely Korean non-profit, MinKwon, registered nearly sixty thousand voters, nearly doubling the percentage of Asians voters in the district and electing its first member of the state assembly.[21] Minority under enrollment is the soft underbelly of Republican hegemony.

## Raising Money

Early in the campaign it is absolutely vital for the candidate and his or her supporters to get around the district and meet with potential supporters. These meet-and-greet sessions are essentially friend-raisers rather than fund-raisers, though the boundaries between the two are not clear. What professional fund-raisers will tell you is that you must first go for the big money with one-on-one contacts. To have a $100 a person event with friends and neighbors who could easily afford to give $2000 lets them off the hook. It is discouraging but true that money counts: in 2018 better than 88 percent of the biggest spenders in House races won and 82 percent in Senate races.[22] Thus one of the first priorities in every campaign is for the candidate to get on the phone and go after the big bucks. The acronym EMILYs List, an organization that supports pro-choice women, stands for "Early Money Is Like Yeast– it makes the dough rise." It is often important in getting the help of organizations and politicians that use a candidate's ability to raise money as a sign of viability. In other words, it takes money to raise money. This is why, "Campaign managers believe that candidates insufficiently committed fundraising are not even worth working for."[23]

In all kinds of ways, small contributors are what you most want, symbolically of course, but also in the very practical sense that the more people who are actively "invested" in a campaign, the greater its potential activist base. The more a campaign relies on a small set of larger donors, conversely, the more vulnerable it is to charges of favoring special interests. Raising money from small donors, however, is seldom efficient. In 2019, when the Democrats used a count of small donors as a standard of qualification for television debates, some candidates spent as much as three or four dollars each from big donors for every dollar they raised through routes such as internet advertising and other ways of making their "small donor quotas. Independent expenditures aside, federal law prohibits any one person from giving more than $2800 to any one campaign, so the number of "large" donors needed is large and explains why any viable candidate must spend hour after hour dialing for dollars. And this money, if it is to attract help from state and national committees, win contributions from ideologically motivated national organizations and individuals, and set up the campaign, must be raised early. Early money is also vital in planning media aspects of a campaign lest the desirable time slots be taken. Catherine Shaw describes a candidate who put off his media buys until October only to find that "basically Saturday cartoons were left."[24] Incumbents have an obvious advantage in accessing early gifts, so do millionaires who can fund their own campaigns. It would be nice to be able to say, as an unsuccessful candidate for mayor of Washington, D. C. once did, that "It's not how much money you raise. It's how you spend your money."[25] In academic terms, most studies show that "there are strongly diminishing marginal returns to campaign spending."[26] But although prudence and care are recommended, under-financed campaigns are almost invariably losing campaigns. Some threshold amount– enough to pay salaries, pay for phone and internet lines, open at least one office, and pay for some form of media– is essentially an entry fee to serious candidacy. For those with a few dollars to donate, the biggest bang for the buck is probably to give a substantial contribution to a candidate in a low income district.

After roughly forty years of almost unchallenged incumbency, Democrats lost their majority in the House of Representatives in 1994. Writing in the wake of that election, Eismer and Pollock presciently observed that,

> Democratic survivors will probably be able to fund adequately their 1996 campaigns. But it will require more hustling, an unappealing prospect that may urge some into retirement. Between defending incumbents and attempting to win back seats lost in 1994, the resources of labor PACs will be stretched very thin. Even with the support of labor PACs, Democrats have lagged behind Republicans in money for challengers.[27]

Especially given the declining financial capacity of organized labor, the question of where new Democratic money comes from is of enduring urgency. It would be nice to be able to say in 2020 that thousands of pissed-off Democrats, minorities, women and gays will pony up and that small donors will tide the party through. As we move in that direction, however, Sutton's Law prevails. When asked why he always robbed banks, the Willie (the Actor) Sutton's reply was "because that's where the money is." And so it is that Democrats must start with those who can most afford to contribute.

Among the straws that broke the back of Hillary Clinton's campaign was the issue of her secret, mega-bucks briefings of such Wall Street giants as Goldman-Sacks. I'd like to think that secrecy was the issue here, and that Clinton handled it badly, but both Sanders and (ironically) Trump managed to make it an issue. The dilemma for Democrats (and apparently not for Republicans) is that the more they observe Sutton's law, the more tarnished their images. With the DNC using the number of small donors reached as part of its 2019-20 matrix for deciding which candidates were qualified for debates, the candidates collectively indeed raised record dollars from record numbers of donors. But it remained the early money that made it possible. What Democrats, particularly at the local level, need to cultivate is a roster of people who can be present at the creation of promising campaigns to provide the jump start that organized labor once provided. It is worth noting, lest we forget, that not all rich people drool and move their lips as they read the Wall Street Journal and watch Fox News. Indeed there are many citizens with substantial resources who are quite liberal, not just on social issues but economic issues as well (e.g., Warren Buffet's lament that his secretary paid income taxes at a higher rate than he does). Well folks, that's where the money is, and the first step in a viable campaign is to find it.    Getting people with money to contribute to a candidate or cause generally involves three steps: first, finding the people who actually have money; second, making the case for them to contribute; and finally, asking. If you get ten people in a room virtually all them will enjoy helping to identify those of their friends and neighbors who have money. Seven or eight out the ten will gladly go out and make the case for the campaign. You are lucky if you can get three who are comfortable doing the actual ask. Often it is more effective to do the "ask" in person with two people– one to make the case, the other to close the deal. The most common mistake people make in asking for money is asking too little. Imagine yourself with a comfortable income, being approached, hearing the pitch, and being asked for five dollars. It's an insult. Ask for two thousand and it's easy for someone to give you a thousand, but almost no one will give you three thousand if you ask for three hundred.

In a district with hundreds of thousands of voters, it is all but impossible for the candidate personally to put the arm on more than a relatively small number of potential voters. Events– from large dinners and rallies to neighborhood "meet and greets"– have the added advantage of giving the candidate exposure, providing the opportunity to recruit new volunteers, and sometimes getting coverage in the media. But these events must be carefully planned. Nothing is more embarrassing than an audience of twenty in a hall that holds two hundred. I personally like the old-fashioned, home-based coffee or cocktail party. An advance person makes a brief pitch, the candidate arrives with an aide, speaks and answers questions for fifteen minutes and is hustled to the next coffee shop, college cafeteria or home; the advance person gets feed-back, makes a pitch for money and volunteers and says good night. A reasonably fit candidate can do ten to fifteen of these events a day. Small events such as these, and direct asks for money have the advantage of being virtually cost free and surprisingly self-sustaining with at least one guest at every coffee klatch offering to host another. And the "ask" can be surprisingly fruitful.

Direct mail and telemarketing campaigns, like registration drives are cost effective in direct relationship to the planning that goes into them, both in targeting potential donors and crafting targeted messages. And they must be carefully targeted to be cost/effective. The internet is much cheaper and many campaigns now prefer it to other media. Hillary Clinton raised roughly a third of her 2016 campaign funds through e-mails. But aside from face-to face appeals, it matters less how potential donors are contacted than whether they were contacted at all. Just as an earlier generation of media targets learned how to ignore political snail mail, and their children found ways to block phone calls, we are reaching a point where the on line trash baskets of voters are beginning to overflow. As anyone who has ever given to a candidate online knows, the more and more desperate pleas of more desperate candidates are becoming easier and easier to ignore, and there is growing evidence that we are reaching a saturation point in the efficacy of such appeals.

If you are lucky, a campaign's pool of volunteers may include a professional fund-raiser and a lawyer or two. If not, it might be wise either to outsource some of the work, or at the least bring in a consultant to work with a local fund-raising team. Targeting, in terms of both audience and media, is an increasingly technical art especially when it comes to fund-raising. Having the endorsements of the local party, and various groups like Emily's list of the National Committee for an Effective Congress can give a campaign access to a lot of professional help with these issues. And of course there are the National and State Party Committees.

The notion that all politics is local is increasingly challenged by our broken system of campaign finance which has both nationalized political money and vastly enhanced the influence of a handful of enormously wealthy families. The three keys to at least partially countering these forces are those of expanding the base of medium and small donors, using resources better, and mobilizing volunteers. The easiest way to channel small donations is through the national, state, House and Senate campaign committees of the Democratic Party; but giving at the local level, where campaigns are, we hope, run in terms of district priorities is far more effective, and has public relations value as well. For those not living in or near competitive campaigns, you can start with the appendices to this book to locate campaigns in your area where you contributions can have an impact. Volunteering your time is even better. Many campaign professionals would agree with Shea and Burton when they argue that, "if a campaign is short on volunteers for a phone bank, it can buy the services of a telemarketing firm; if, however, the campaign is short on money, volunteers will not pay the long-distance bill."[28] This was written more than a decade ago; but even then I would suggest that a campaign that was spending it on telemarketing firms would not get my money. And the simple fact is that volunteers are not only of value in themselves but often become motivated financial resources. Both volunteering and contributing tend to give those who donate a stake in the outcome. What substantial financial bases in the district give to campaigns is autonomy.

Expanding the base of small donors, particulalry at the ditrict level, is also a key step in Congressional reform. It is absolutely vital to divorce the distribution of positions and influence in Congress from campaign finance. In both parties, members of the House and Senate are expected to spend a day a week "dialing for dollars," funds– beyond use for their own campaigns– that go to the party leaders to recruit new candidates and support incumbents who will support the party line. Beyond that, committee and leadership positions come with a price: to be chairman or ranking minority member of a key committee you must raise at least a quarter of a million dollars for the party. Given the stacking of the Supreme Court, there is no realistic chance of repealing *Citizens United* or the equally odious

*McCutcheon v. FEC* but the Democrats can unilaterally reform their own rules of the campaign finance game and still win elections. The congressional campaign committees need to have the resources to go into districts where local sources of campaign funds are hard to find; but the key to real reform still lies in putting people into politics and campaigning at the street level.

## Hunting Butterflies

In the 1790s, Thomas Jefferson and James Madison traveled through the northeast allegedly collecting butterflies. What they were actually collecting were the allies and friends who became the core of what is now the Democratic Party. I don't think anybody knows what kinds of lists they came north with, but you can be sure that they knew in advance who they wanted to talk with and who they did not. Good politics begins with good lists.

The national committees and the senatorial and congressional campaign committees are, as we noted in chapter 2, increasingly involved in compiling, refining and sharing data bases. Nothing is more central to a successful campaign. Computers have revolutionized political lists, allowing a super-segmentation of voter lists and an ever-increasing ability to micro-target fund-raising, media and get-out the vote efforts. In its essence, however, it remains both a traditional science and art of trying to determine in advance what voters are most and least likely to vote for your candidate. What Issenberg calls the "hard ID" voters, those who have explicitly told a canvasser or caller for whom they will vote, are still the gold standard of all campaigns. "But no campaign," as he points out, "has ever been able to hard-ID every voter in the universe, or even a majority of them."[29] Not only are the costs prohibitive, but even self-reported voting intentions are not completely reliable. Out of a desire to be friendly, or out of simple perversity, people lie. They also change their minds. In fact, since the early voting behavior studies of the 1960s, many political scientists have actually been able to predict how people will vote with greater accuracy than have the voters themselves. In the 2016 elections, models based on demographic factors and past election returns often turned out to be more likely accurately to predict Donald Trump's victory than the polls that asked people who they intended to support.

As noted in chapter 2, what modern campaign consultants have been able to do is to accumulate multiple years of polls and canvas results and write "statistical algorithms based on known information about a small set of voters," and use these to "extrapolate to find other voters who looked– and presumably thought and acted– like them, treating "these virtual IDs as an effective replacement for hard IDs where it couldn't get them."[30] Beyond poll results, the computer models can suck up reams of individualized data from motor vehicle ownership to military service. It can tell you who subscribes to what magazines and newspapers, gives to some charities, and (in some states) are registered to carry firearms. It can include lists of everyone who has given more than $100 to a national political campaign. Not all suburban, Italian-American drivers of Dodge Ram trucks who shop at Walmart and play fantasy football vote the same way, and that may not be a usable category; but the more narrowly focused each statistical type becomes through testing and retesting, the closer each virtual ID can be used to replace a hard one. And even fairly simple algorithms can be enormously useful as, for example, by soliciting money only from those who are registered Democrats who have given previously, you can save a ton of money in postage.

It is difficult not to feel some discomfort with the idea of "managing" voters by targeting communications and ignoring the masses. It too easily conjures images of creating managed citizens.[31] Given that the other side is also becoming more adept at mobilizing their supporters, micro targeting can only exacerbate polarization. In many ways, however, these fears are overblown. Writing about the Obama campaign's use of these algorithms Kreiss argues that critics "generally overstate the control that campaign staffers and political consultants have over the electorate." Its use of computational management of an increasingly sophisticated data base, its

> Control of supporters' actions was always probabilistic not deterministic. Control was limited to increasing the likelihood that people would take particular actions for the campaign. It was confined to easily measured domains, such as sign-ups to the e-mail list and donations. While the campaign used data to coordinate its volunteers and new media applications . . . there was plenty of volunteer agency in the interstices of these systems.[32]

The role of volunteers is absolutely crucial in filling these gaps between computer models and real, as opposed to virtual citizens. That kind of volunteer agency, moreover, is far more efficacious. Both New Jersey and New York had local elections in 2019 where they had access to the Democratic Party's lists and, in many towns, the lists kept from the 2018 canvasses for Malinowski and Delgado. In both campaigns, the actual lists identified as many twice as many likely Democratic voters as did the virtual lists.

In the best case, the lists compiled going door to door also compile contact information which can then be used to reinforce the connection. With a phone number or e-mail address, a personal visit can be preceded or followed up the next day with a text message reinforcing the message with a text that comes from a recognized person. A loophole in in the laws regulating telecommunications now allows sending texts to thousands of strangers, to the point where some voters are getting literally dozens of get-out-vote and other messages from campaigns that are thousands of miles a way. Yours may well join them in trash unless your contact is expecting to hear from you.

The most important role of local volunteers is to provide ongoing human feedback to the computer models. Even as American voters have become more polarized, there is still an enormous amount of slack and dynamism in the system. All the campaign manuals you might buy, for example, will tell you not to bother knocking on the doors of registered, regular voters of the opposition party. And this is generally true in the weeks before the election when your presence might actually remind them to vote. But putting people back in politics means reinstating the old machine politician's knack for both mobilizing voters and using volunteers to listen to what rank-and-file voters are saying. And while political polarization is a fact of life, a very large slice of the electorate remains uncommited with their partisan identities relatively fluid. The "big surprise" of the 2016 presidential election was, supposedly, how many white, working class, usually-Democratic voters went for Trump. Of equal, though less noticed, magnitude was the switch of suburban women to the Democrats, and the long-range move of Asians and Hispanics toward the Party. Dr. Murphy's follow-up study of the effects of the anti-war student involvement in campaigns in the 1970s, found "preference increases" of between 3.9 and 17.2% among contacted voters.33 Voters may well be more set in their opinions than they were in the days of the Viet Nam war, but the point is that there is still enough slack in the system that voter preferences– especially when prodded through face-to-face contact– may be more fungible than many professional practitioners may think. The fight over impeachment, and the misfeasances of Donald Trump it revealed may have hardened attitudes toward Republicans in some cases, or shaken them up in largely unpredictable ways.

Let's get back to picking cherries. Registration lists and past voting records are the time-tested starting points, but they are by no means definitive. There are more people who refuse to identify themselves with either party than as Republicans or Democrats. Data bases can show which of these voters are inclined to vote one way or the other, but there are still large numbers who cannot be classified. Of those registered with a party, moreover, many are partisans in disguise. And with those who are registered with parties, many are there more from habit than conviction. The most effective way of identifying who is who is to ask. At their best, the most sophisticated computer models serve as guidelines not manuals. They identify where cherry trees are likely to be found, not where they actually are. And they can be badly misused.

For many years, for example, campaigns would buy or compile lists of "prime voters," those who had long histories of regularly voting in party primaries and general elections. While it cannot hurt to remind people that there is an election coming up, and while it makes sense to aim campaign literature at those most likely to vote, you are in a general sense preaching to the choir. Even the more sophisticated lists of the DNC are designed to identify people who are already those most likely to vote, and to vote Democratic. The cherries that need to be picked to win in marginal districts, however, are those who are not dedicated partisans. As statistical models are refined and improved, they will increasingly able to differentiate these voters as well, but will never do so as well as can actual face-to-face communications. Party generated lists can be particularly useful in the efficient targeting of mail and other media, but even here targeting founded in face-to-face, two-way conversations wins.

## Spending Money

Here's the deal: before you spend a nickel in a campaign, you must set your priorities. This is, essentially, the job of a professional campaign manager. But just as he or she might be considered both the CEO and CFO of the campaign (not to mention the candidate) there should be some kind of executive committee to help set priorities. It has been said that half of the money spent in the typical campaign is wasted, the problem is that we don't know which half.

Generally campaigns work through four overlapping stages: enrollment, identification, persuasion and mobilization. Voters must first be registered and volunteers signed up, they must know who the candidate is and for what office, persuaded to vote for him or her, and finally reminded actually to cast a ballot. The enrollment stage, registering voters and signing up volunteers is actually continuous and cannot be started too early. Nor can it ever be too early to begin opposition research, organization, fund-raising and mapping the district. All of this work essentially is conducted one-on-one and behind the scenes.

The starting point of the public campaign is to gain name recognition as the base point for establishing connections. Yard signs, bumper stickers, buttons and billboards are traditional vehicles that put names in play and hopefully link them to a more general campaign motif such as party affiliation, a slogan or just a color scheme that will run through the weeks ahead. Studies have shown that randomly placed get-out-the-vote signs increase turnout by a percentage or two. People who display lawn signs are more likely to vote than those who don't, and there may even be some modest effects on candidate preferences. They are also expensive, particularly signs which are increasingly likely to be stolen or defaced. The very tech savvy people in Obama's campaign were skeptical enough of the efficacy of these devices that they essentially treated them more as aspects of the fund-raising efforts than advertising. In local races– particularly in those that rely heavily on volunteers– signs, enough at least to match the opposition, may be needed to keep up morale, and buttons may be useful in opening doors. Every campaign must have at least one basic brochure. Some advertising is necessary if only to give volunteers and contributors a sense of seriousness. And if radio, television and print media are cost effective, money should be set aside for professional production costs. To spend a few thousand dollars producing an ad that costs hundreds of thousands to broadcast is throwing money away.

Paid media move up from name recognition to persuasion. Increasingly, campaign professionals are moving from general media to those more narrowly focused, finding the best media for reaching which groups. To take an obvious example, you don't buy time on hip hop radio stations to pitch your position on Medicare. Then there are questions of cost-effectiveness. A candidate running for congress in southern California who buys ad time on a Los Angeles television station is either very rich or desperate as he or she is covering the costs of a message that will appear in 24 other districts. This is not the place for a detailed analysis of these questions, particularly since they will differ markedly from one type of district to another. But the under-lying rule is simple: media choices should be made not because this is the way it has always been done, but out of a shrewd calculation as to how cost-effectively they can reach your voter base. Issenberg credits Republican strategist Timmy Teepill with thinking "of politics not as an activity conducted in well-bounded geographic spaces but as one that pulsed through networks of people linked by common interests."[33] Old media people thought of cost-effectiveness in terms of "CPMs," or costs per thousands of people reached. In the new politics it is who gets reached, with what, through what media and at what cost.

With any media you are in competition not with the opposition so much as with every commodity and cause targeting the same audience. We are all good at ignoring the hundreds of messages beamed at us daily by people who are experts at getting our attention. So when the candidate's carefully crafted flyer arrives in the mailbox, it probably arrives with an equally alluring ad from a real estate agent, a piece from a dentist offering a better smile, and a sure cure for hemorrhoids. So unless your hemorrhoids are acting up or you are in the market for a new house, all four brochures probably go into the trash. So whether your media of choice is direct mail, the internet, TV, or radio it must be both targeted and able to penetrate our skepticism. It must also be suited to the medium: your wonderfully-crafted video will look very different on a hand-held screen (where more than half of its viewers will see it) than on a big screen television.

The internet, particularly e-mails specifically targeted to individuals, has the potential to turn old rules on their heads. In particular, it can personalize contacts, providing opportunities, virtually unavailable through traditional media, for communications that listen to voters at the same as you try to influence them, getting instant feedback on what works and what doesn't, and genuinely giving people a sense of being involved in the campaign. Not the least, the new media provide opportunities to make large numbers of volunteers partners in the campaign. But please, avoid the temptation– because it only takes a few clicks– to overload inboxes with the electronic equivalent of junk mail. Simple hint: people always open emails from people they know.

## Winning Votes

What most campaign consultants insist from the outset is that a campaign stay on message. "It's the economy, stupid," it said on signs posted all over Bill Clinton's campaign offices in 1994 as a reminder not to get side-tracked. Ideally, it is argued, everything the campaign does should be considered through the lens of an over-arching theme: green yard signs if the environment is the issue, blue signs and Democrat in big letters if the party match is good. Out of necessity and choice, most modern campaigns run wholesale, one major central supplier working through a spotty network of retail vote seekers, relying largely on paid media to push the product. Mobilization not conversion, getting your voters to the polls is the norm.

But although Democrats are the majority party, skewed demographics, voting rules, gerrymandering and the lower turnout rates of the party's supporters necessitate extra effort. The most sophisticated election analysts– such as Rasmussen, Sabato, Rothenberg and Abramowitz– suggest that Democrats needed to increase their overall popular vote by at least seven per cent in order to gain their majority in the House in 2018. They must retain that margin in 2020. And because so many of the Republican seats up in 2020 are in red states it will take at least that much of surge in the Senate. The twin keys to gaining such a margin are in the areas of voter registration and getting out the vote; but working with Democrats alone will probably not suffice. Going after independents– who are generally less sophisticated and less informed voters– is tricky but necessary. Even more than with party stalwarts, the efforts must be clearly targeted both in terms of voters and messages. We have seen how increasingly sophisticated surveys and computer algorithms have enabled candidates to target individual voters. They are also getting more sophisticated in telling us how to package the campaign message: what issues, especially should be emphasized with what voters. This is not to say that a candidate's stands on issues should be driven by polls, in fact if there is anything worse than being out of step with the voters it coming across as phony or slick. What it most certainly does mean is being able to craft the campaign message in terms of local concerns and circumstances. What works in California may not work in Texas, and the more that national figures attempt to define the issues of the year, the more it may behoove local candidates to assert their independence.

Here again, the heavy hand of Supreme Court's campaign finance decisions have a major impact. Under current law, major contributors, while they are still marginally constrained in helping individual candidates may make virtually unlimited, virtually anonymous contributions to independent committees. In 2012 alone, one study found, nearly one billion dollars that could not legally have been spent in 2008 was used by such outside groups to influence the election.[34] Aside from the enormous distorting influence of such money on the whole political process, a less noticed but also significant impact of these independent expenditures lies in their impact on individual campaigns which are increasingly less in control of their own messages. By law, the only limit on these groups is that their expenditures are totally uncoordinated with the campaign. Whether voters know that or not, your message may not be in your hands.

What are in your hands are the messages you send. For many voters, their contact with a volunteer may be virtually the only campaign message they attend to. The content of political messages is going to vary much according to local conditions and—especially with campaigns run largely by volunteers—in response to the feedback that constituents provide. A few of the guidelines that might prove useful are the following: first, and most obviously, the media world has changed. Newspapers do have the advantage of communicating with opinion leaders and although they become increasingly less cost-effective as Election Day nears, their endorsements help. And in local markets, it doesn't hurt to put in a few paid advertisements. Television remains a powerful medium and even if at least half of the time they will be viewed on a hand-held screen or in a tavern where the sound is turned off, the power of strong visuals is enormous. Why so many candidates still produce talking head commercials, or spend thousands buying time to show poorly produced spots is beyond me. Television can also be prohibitively expensive when candidates are paying for markets that include many other districts, or when the time buys are made too late in the campaign to be effectively placed. Radio has similar cost inefficiencies, but has the advantage of playing to much more clearly segmented audiences. Campaigns often forget that all of these media are often hungry for good local content news, sending a brief clip for the evening news is like getting free advertising. With all of these media, the biggest mistake of most campaigns is to focus more on coverage than content. A really effective commercial that airs less frequently is better than a bad one endlessly repeated. It is ironic but true that most candidates will spend more time preparing a speech before sixty Rotary Club members than working on a commercial or press release that will be seen by thousands. Every candidate, moreover, should have a short, well-thought-out statement on all of the dozen or so issues likely to arise at candidate forums or in contacts with the media. Nothing is more embarrassing than a candidate hemming and hawing on the evening news.

In the long run, or crudely done, as distasteful as negative commercials often are, most studies clearly show that they work. Perhaps the best way of going negative without feeling a little dirty, is to avoid direct attacks. Tony Schwartz's "daisy" ad for Lyndon Johnson in 1964 was shown only once, but may be the most famous political ad ever run. It showed a little girl counting the petals of a daisy. With her count morphing into a countdown, the girl's image faded into the mushroom cloud of a nuclear bomb. "The stakes are high," the screen read, "Vote for Johnson." The ad was bitterly criticized by many who said that the ad unfairly attacked Johnson's opponent as a dangerous warmonger. But as Schwartz pointed out, the ad said nothing about Barry Goldwater, what it did with the images was to resonate with ideas about Senator Goldwater that were already in peoples' heads. And that truly is one of the best ideas in all kinds of political advertising, and it underlines the importance of polling and other forms of feedback—especially that from volunteers going door-to-door– to find out what's in people's heads and how each message from the campaign can be made to resonate with it.

One final point on content. Gloom and doom ads may work in the short run, and running against Congress (while running for it) is popular even among incumbents. Aside from the systemic effects of such campaigns, the danger is that they threaten to depress turnout, even in the short run. And depressing turnout hurts Democrats. If the system is as dysfunctional as many Americans already believe, what is the sense in participating in its rituals? The real issue is not one of changing the basic system but of changing the people who are causing it to fail.

## Get Out the Vote

No matter how good the message, how efficient the campaign, the bottom line is getting out your vote on or before Election Day. The GOTV effort, coincidentally, is the campaign arena in which volunteers able to have their greatest impact. Virtually all campaign professionals agree that with good lists going door to door is the single most effective way to get out the vote. As Green and Gerber put it,

> The more personal the interaction between campaign and potential voter, the more it raises a person's chances of voting. Door-to-door canvassing by enthusiastic volunteers is the gold-standard mobilization tactic; chatty, unhurried phone calls seem to work well too. Automatically dialed, prerecorded GOTV phone calls, by contrast, are utterly impersonal and, evidently, wholly ineffective at getting people to vote.[35]

This is one area of campaign management that has been systematically studied, and virtually every field experiment comparing the use of different methods has confirmed Green and Gerber's basic finding The effects, moreover, can be quite substantial, adding as much or more than seven percent to a candidate's vote total. Compiling numerous GOTV studies, moreover, Green and Gerber were able to compare the relative cost-effectiveness of various ways of trying to affect turnout such as leafleting (which had trivial effects), robo calls (none), direct mail (trivial), targeted phone calls by trained volunteers (good), and so on. This analysis is must reading for any campaign team. Effective get out the vote drives are founded in sound research, with algorithms or, preferably, the results of canvassing. They are premised on the time tested notions that mobilizing your latent supporters is much more efficient than converting others, and that attempts to convert close to Election Day may have the contrary effect of turning out the opposition.

The basic canvass identifying sure and likely supporters, is done before Election Day. Thirty-three states now allow early voting, and almost a third of the voters in those states have availed themselves of that opportunity, so it is crucial to know what the deadlines and procedures are. Most states also allow absentee ballots which also have application and submission deadlines. The opportunities these procedures open are enormous, most obviously in contained communities such as retirement homes and college dormitories. Volunteers cannot only help residents apply for ballots, but make follow-up calls to make sure that people actually vote. Knowing who has actually voted, moreover, sharply eases the GOTV work needed on Election Day.

Targeting and records of which voters have already cast their ballots in hand, what happens on Election Day is perhaps most crucial. Whether because of a fight with the boss or a hot date, the chances are that some people will simply forget to vote. For political activists and candidates that Tuesday may be New Years, Thanksgiving and the Fourth of July rolled into one, but for most voters it's just another Tuesday. All of your work may go for naught unless and until you close the deal on this one day. First thing in the morning, at every polling place, there should be a volunteer. Every party on the ballot (or every candidate in a primary) is entitled to sit behind or beside the official election judges ostensibly to challenge fraudulent voters, but largely, in practice, as the major component of the GOTV effort. There should be three lists of registered voters with the names of those who have already cast and early or absentee ballot crossed off and a contact number and/or e-mail address. (Some states do the work of listing those who have voted for you). As each new voter appears, his or her name is crossed off until about two hours before the polls close when a runner should be dispatched to take one of the lists to people manning a phone (or standing in a nearby public area using their cell phones). Any of your candidate's identified supporters should then be contacted and reminded to vote. An hour later, the revised second list is used to again contact those who haven't voted. Being able to provide a ride may be particularly important for seniors, the disabled, and those living in remote areas, a providing a few minutes of child care can also be much appreciated. That's it. Simple as it sounds this tried and trusted election-day routine generally can be counted on to add at least ten or fifteen voters to the total in each precinct.

## The Anatomy of Victory

For all the research that has been done by political scientists, pollsters, campaign consultants and statisticians, campaigns and elections are as much art as science. We know a lot about how voters decide and about how those decisions can be influenced. But there is a lot that we don't. What we do know can be summarized in pretty simple terms. First, nothing works better than personal contact. Getting the candidate out and around is the starting point, putting real people on the ground is far and away the next best thing. Second, it is easier and generally more effective to influence who actually votes than how they vote. Of all the things an individual can do to change the face of American politics, the easiest and most effective is that of getting like-minded individuals to vote. Money is, of course, important in politics, but we know a lot less about the effects of campaign spending than we do about the impact of volunteers.

> Direct mobilization in the form of party and candidate contact significantly increases the extent to which most citizens are familiar with the candidates in congressional races and increases the extent to which citizens are able to place the candidates on an ideological scale. Further, direct mobilization appears to have a much greater effect than candidate spending. Indeed candidate spending may even have a negative effect.[36]

It is certainly easier to go on line and make a campaign contribution. It may be even more effective to talk with your neighbors. Although the populations of formal precincts or voting districts vary, if you drew your own map of neighborhoods of say two hundred and fifty voters each, and if a thousand volunteers covering those of areas could persuade just ten new people to register and vote, if their GOTV work has the typical effect of turning out ten more, that's a minimum swing of 20,000 votes. There are nearly twenty congressional districts where that amount of extra Democratic votes changed the outcome in 2018, and where similar statewide surges in 2016 would have won Clinton the presidency in a landslide. Volunteers can make the difference. It should also be noted that these contacts often have cumulative effects in the sense that they often discover other potential volunteers and financial donors. There are no better ways of building an organization. Finally, a campaign that begins its strategic planning with a focus on a precinct-by-precinct ground game can develop increasingly efficient targeted media campaigns around them. Technology and shoe leather combined can win a simple campaign trifecta by using the information fed back from canvassers to targeted media. Consider this possible scenario: on Sunday, the campaign worker contacts voter X who, in the course of conversation, indicates a particular interest in climate change. The volunteer, offering a more detailed report on the candidate's position gets the voter's e-mail. On Monday the follow-up response– from the volunteer but with a message from the candidate– is in the voter's inbox. On Wednesday– by special arrangement with a USPS service that promises delivery of campaign material on a specified date– the voter gets a flyer in the mail touting the candidate and emphasizing environmental issues. You can even follow up with an e-mail asking for money or time. And on Election Day, this is one of the voters you remind. This is what post-modern politics is all about.

# Endnotes

1   Sassha Issenberg, The Victory Lab: The Secret Science of Winning Campaigns (New York: Broadway Books, 2013), 68.

2   Brian J. Box, Back in the Game: Political Party Campaigning in the Era of Reform (Albany: State University of New York Press, 3013). 10.

3   Milton Rakove, Don't Make No Waves. . . Don't Back No Losers: An Insider's Analysis of the Daley Machine (Bloomington: Indiana University Press), 96.

4   Ibid., 97.

5   On the measurement and history of polarization see Sean M. Theriault, Party Polarization in Congress (New York: Cambridge University Press, 2008).

6   The only systematic work I know of is the rather dated summary in David A. Leuthold, Electioneering in a Democracy (New York: John Wiley and Sons, 1994). More recent polls and the websites of groups are less systematic but generally list the same general attributes.

7   Ibid.

8   Naomi Klein, No Is Not Enough: Rethinking Trumps' Shock Politics and Winning the World We Need (Chicago: Haymarket Books, 2017), 42.

9   Elaine C. Camarck, Increasing Turnout in Congressional Primaries (Washington, DC: The Brookings Institution Center for Effective Public Management, 2014), 8.

10  Michael Walzer, Political Action: A Practical Guide to Movement Politics (Chicago: Quadrangle Books, 1971), 40.

11   James Q. Wilson, The Amateur Democrat: Club Politics in Three Cities (Chicago: University of Chicago Press, 1970).

12  U. S. Census Bureau, Reported Voting and Registration by Race, Hispanic Origin, Sex and Age, November 2016. https://census.gov/data/tables/time-series/demo/voting-and-registration/p20-53. Accessed September 10, 2019.

13  Ibid.

14  Susan Mizner and Eric Smith, Access Denied: Barriers to Online Voter Registration for Citizens with Disabilities (New York: American Civil Liberties Union, 2015).

15  Anthony Downs, An Economic Theory of Democracy (New York: Harper and Row, 1961), 123.

16  Lyn Ragsdale and Jerrold G. Rusk, The American Nonvoter (New York: Oxford University Press, 2017), 24.

17  Isenberg, 314.

18  The study can be found at http.//www.pewtrusts.org/en/research-and-analysis/issue-briefs/2017/06/why-are-millions-of-citizens-not-mot-registered. Accessed, December 29, 2018.

19  William T. Murphy, Jr. and Edward Schneier, Vote Power: How to Work for the Person You Want Elected (Garden City, NY: Anchor Book, 1974), 107

20  Heath Brown, Immigrants and Electoral Politics: Nonprofit Organizations in a Time of Demographic Change (Ithaca, NY: Cornell University Press, 2016), 2.

21  Center for Responsive Politics, "Did Money Win?" http://www.opensecrets.org/electons-overview//Did-money-win?

22  William J. Feltus, Kenneth M. Goldstein and Matthew Dallek, Inside Campaigns: Elections through the Eyes of Political Professionals (Washington: CQ Press, 2nd ed., 2019), 81.

23  Catherine Shaw, The Campaign Manager: Running and Winning Local Elections (Boulder, CO: Westview Press, fifth ed.; 2014), 114.

24  Jeffrey Gildenhorn as quoted in Shaw, 121.

25  Jeff Milyo, "Campaign Spending and Electoral Competition: Towards More Policy Relevant Research," The Forum: A Journal of Applied Research on Contemporary Politics (2013), 37.

26  Theodore J. Eismeier and Phillip H. Pollock III, "Money in the 1994 Elections and Beyond," in Phillip A. Klinker, ed., The Elections of 1994 in Context (Boulder, CO: Westview Press, 1996), 95.

27  Daniel M. Shea and Micheal John Burton, Campaign Craft: The Strategies, Tactics and Art of Political Campaign Management (Westport, CT: Praeger, 2006), 12.

28  Issenberg, 248.

29  Ibid.

30  Victoria Carry, Wired and Mobilizing: Social Movements, New Technology and Electoral Politics (New York: Routledge, 2010).

31  Donald Kreiss, Taking Our Country Back: The Crafting of Networked Politics from Howard Dean to Barak Obama (New York: Oxford University Press, 2012). 195.

32  Murphy and Schneier, 66.

33  Issenberg, 102.

34  Conor M. Dowling and Michael G. Miller, eds., Super PAC! Money, Elections and Voters After Citizens United (New York: Routledge, 2014), 7.

35  Donald P. Green and Alan S. Gerber, Get Out the Vote: How to Increase Voter Turnout (Washington: The Brookings Institution, 3rd ed., 2015), 9.

36  Roberta K. Goidel, Donald A. Gross and Todd G. Shields, Money Matters: Consequences of Campaign Reform in U. S. House Races (Lanham, MD: Rowman and Littlefield, 1999), 135-36.

---

——◆——— **Chapter 4** ———◆———

# Advocacy

*Executive Summary and Action Plan*

People become involved in politics largely because they are concerned about issues. They can have an impact by various forms "agitation," such as demonstrations; by lobbying public officials; and by working in campaigns. In campaigns one of the most difficult problems many activists have is that of seeing issues as tools for electoral victory and future compromise rather than as ends in themselves. In a complex democracy no candidate for any office– not for President, nor Freeholder, State Senator, Sheriff nor Member of Congress– will ever have his or her program enacted precisely into law. It is disingenuous, deceitful, dangerous, and all too common to pretend otherwise.

Agitation too is a strategy that has higher expectations and fewer constraints. Its purpose is to express opinions in the hope of changing others. Unlike lobbying, which focuses on the details of policy, the point of demonstrations, media campaigns, and so on is to change the political agenda, bring particular issues to the forefront, engage activists and impact public perceptions. It can also serve as a terrific tool for bringing like-minded people together. It would be difficult to over-estimate how important the January 2018 Women's Marches were in bringing people together for successful election campaigns later in the year.

Because the 2020 elections will leave conservatives able to block many significant changes, the immediate focus must be on elections and agitation to replace an ideologically-driven politics of negativism and irrationality with the kind of pluralistic checks and balances established by the Founders. The interest groups politics that long biased the system toward the more affluent was clearly flawed; but it was at the same time more vulnerable to ordinary citizens and far more democratic than one dominated by a handful of largely anonymous donors. Progressive advocacy efforts must per force be aimed at campaigns and agitation looking both toward and beyond 2020. Restoring a viable pluralism and rationality in politics begins with the election of representatives who have a genuine interest in issues and whose base of support is at the grassroots. Many progressives are appropriately skeptical of interest group politics and the lobbying that sustains it; but while it has, and, honestly, usually will have an upper-class bias it is the only viable way of bringing some sort of balance to the system.

## Elections, Issues, Agitation and Lobbying

Every legislative campaign should have people working on issues, on the one hand in opposition research that looks at where other candidates stand; and, on the other hand, at how the aspirations of candidates and voters are best defined and explained in terms of good public policy, good politics, and feasibility. Briefing sheets (note the root word "brief") should be provided to everyone going door-to-door. Every good candidate should be prepared to have something brief but intelligent to say about almost every issue likely to arise. Many Republicans in 2018 hurt themselves badly by refusing to attend town meetings or any unscripted events. Smart politicians welcome almost all communications from constituents as opportunities to sample public attitudes and to put their own spin on their replies and– above all– to feed the data base. To duck an issue or avoid questions is to let others define the meaning of your silence. As obvious as this sounds, there are a growing number of campaigns that isolate their candidates in an attempt to stay rigidly focused "on message." That message, in turn is all too often generated from outside of the district.

The Republican candidates in 2018 who avoided public meetings and sessions with the press lost both in negative publicity and in perceptions of character. In *The Federalist*, Number 57, Madison argued that the aim of the

Constitution was to obtain rulers "who possess most wisdom to discern, and most virtue to pursue, the common good," and, "to take the most effectual precautions to for keeping them virtuous whilst they continue to hold their public trust." The Constitution he went on, provided the means of securing "their fidelity to their constituents." First was the simple fact of their election, of being freely chosen by their fellow citizens "under circumstances which cannot fail to produce a temporary affection at least" to them. Through frequent elections, moreover, they would develop "an habitual recollection of their dependence on the people." And this is how– when our system is working as the Founders intended– we keep our representatives honest and accountable. You develop a legislator's "temporary affection" by being a vital part of his or her election team; he or she develops "an habitual recollection" of this relationship by maintaining those ties.

As party discipline and central agenda control have increased, particularly among House Republicans, individual candidates have been less able to develop relationships of this kind. In what they call "cartel politics" Cox and McCubbins argue that individual legislators have increasingly sacrificed their own control over campaign issues to support for the "party brand."[1] Party leaders control the legislative agenda by only bringing issues to the floor that have been crafted to unite the party's members as a whole, and by not allowing votes on issues that might divide them. In both parties, moreover, there is increasing pressure to toe the party line through the aggressive use of committee assignments and other rewards as well as through their influence on potential campaign donors. Major donors and ideological groups have also tended further to nationalize legislative campaigns. Progressive Democrats, for example, have shown a growing willingness to challenge moderates not only in primaries but even in supporting third party spoilers. So-called "independent expenditures," virtually untouched by campaign finance limits, have increasingly found wealthy conservatives like the Koch brothers and liberal groups like the League of Conservation Voters spending an increasing proportion of overall campaign dollars, much of it in primaries. House elections, however, continue to be won or lost in 435 separate districts, and Senate elections in 50 states which, when well organized, can provide walls of insulation from these nationalizing forces.

The steps that campaign volunteers can take in helping candidates win can become the first steps in longer advocacy efforts. Among campaign volunteers, one will almost invariably find a surprising range of policy "experts:" teachers with strong ideas on educational issues, health care workers who understand how the system can be improved, highways workers and maintenance people with ideas on infrastructure. Going to local experts– school teachers, small business people, drug and alcohol counselors, first responders, union leaders, health care professionals, and so on– can be both informative and a useful way of campaigning. People rather like to talk about themselves and what they are doing. The point here, however, is home-grown advocacy networks growing out of these campaign panels can later compete with national lobbying organizations in keeping members up to date.

It is in their perceptions of the role of issues in campaigns that volunteers and professionals have been most likely to conflict. Professionals view issues more as tools than ends in themselves. It is not that they want candidates to lie or say things they don't mean, but their focus is on deciding questions of tone and emphasis almost entirely in terms of their electoral impact. The signs saying, "It's the economy stupid" that hung on every wall in Bill Clinton's campaign for President were there to remind the candidate and everyone working for him of the importance of staying on message. This can be difficult for many activists accept, and is indeed one of the aspects of modern campaigns that has turned many activists away. The person who volunteers to work for a candidate largely out of a concern for, say, immigration issues, will likely find the campaign's downplaying of those issues a bitter pill to swallow. Yet if all the polls and focus groups show that other issues are the ones resonating with most voters, you had to be prepared to take the pill. In a post-modern campaign, election is still the primary goal, but through its ability to focus on segments of the electorate as opposed to a media market focusing on the whole district, it can accommodate more than one or two issues at a time. Clinton, and most modern, media-oriented candidates aimed their campaigns at the lowest common denominator, the single bullet issue that could reach the most voters. The personalized approach of face-to-face campaigns can, as the old saying goes, accommodate different strokes for different folks. And even in districts that are not reached by volunteers, there are data services available that can allow campaigns to target diverse issue groups.

But as important as issues are in campaigns and elections, issue advocacy is not the same as campaigning. Campaigns are about changing the people who govern, advocacy is about changing their ideas. Certainly there is overlap. When I was an officer of the Princeton Community Democratic Organization in the 1960s we refused to endorse a candidate for the County Board of Chosen Freeholders because he refused to say he opposed the war in Viet Nam. "What the hell does the war have to do with county government?" he asked. It goes to character, was the best I could reply. I still believe that our stand served a political end: indeed within a year our newly elected Freeholder changed his position on the War as opinion more generally shifted and as the impact of federal budget priorities increasingly impacted county government. A decade later, conversely, long before its time, the Downtown Independent Democrats (DID) in lower Manhattan voted not to endorse any primary candidate who opposed gay rights. I think it made a difference in our liberal district and in the liberal borough of Manhattan; but our position was much less sustainable when it came to city and state-wide elections where few candidates had even thought about the issue. We could and did raise it with them, and that was important; but how could we remain neutral even in our own congressional district when a progressive candidate, who was with us on every other issue, refused to accept our stand on gay rights (which his opponent was even more actively against)? We changed our policy. There are times for agitation and times for pragmatism. Different groups and different individuals will draw the line at different times and on different issues. On the War in the 1970s, the nation was at a turning point. The problem, we thought, was to swing the entire direction of national debate, to shape, in particular, the position of the Democratic Party. On gay rights, the problem was not yet one of mass mobilization or national debate— we hoped that would come in the future— but of simply getting the issue on the political agenda. We were in effect starting the conversation on what turned out to be a long, and still ongoing battle. But in that particular time and place, when a major policy shift on the issue was unlikely, it made no sense to abandon whatever influence we might have had on other issues.

Agitation is a strategy not an end. There are times and issues, too long ignored, that need to be brought to the forefront. Nationally, it is important to keep progressive dialogue alive and to use the period leading up to November 2020 to refine and seek consensus on issues like immigration and the environment. If these issues are not ready for prime time in the electoral arena (neither was frequently mentioned in the 2018 campaigns), they can be advanced the broader court of public opinion and Congress. What the Democrats can do leading up to 2020 is to keep raising these issues as they move toward a consensus on concrete policy proposals that will shape the agenda for debate. Both as House members 2019-20 and as candidates in 2020, Democratic members of Congress can contrast themselves with many Republicans by welcoming town hall meetings and legislative hearings openly to discuss these issues. Whether a Democratic President and Congress ultimately agree on Medicare for all or some other plan, the dialogue on the left must be civil and focused on, at the very least, retaining and hopefully extending the gains of the Obama years. What it must not be is an intolerant attempt to impose an ideology on all Democrats in fifty diverse states.

Agitation is not the same as lobbying. In the 1970s we had no concrete plan as to how we would extract the nation from the War. Even in liberal Manhattan forty years ago, we were talking about discrimination not gay marriage or the rights of the transgendered. The whole point of agitation is more one of raising questions than of providing answers. Answers are what elections and lobbyists provide. The goal of advocacy is to shape the political agenda, to establish in general terms the issues to be considered and the problems to be debated. Lobbying deals with specific solutions to those problems.

2020 appears as if it will tilt more toward agenda setting than problem solving. Even if Democrats win the presidency, retain a majority in the House and score an upset in the Senate, the margins will be too small for more than a handful of significant policy initiatives. To those whose energy is directed toward a single-payer system, or a comprehensive and effective program for combating climate change, the short run answer is: not yet. Significant change is not going to come until we are in, or on the cusp of a major realigning period, and using these issues toward that end is a realistic long-range goal. The larger the progressive margins in 2020, the more progress toward these goals is possible. Nothing will happen, however, unless progressive issue advocates think in terms agitation and education *plus* electability. The specifics will come later. More importantly, there can be little substantive progress on any of these issues absent legislative reforms that enable the Congress to recapture its Article I Constitutional control over the lawmaking process. The first step here is simply that of electing legislators with genuine interests in legislation.

## The Party System and the Pressure System

In a classic textbook, the late V. O. Key defined pressure groups as groups that "promote their interests by attempting to influence government rather than by nominating candidates and seeking responsibility for the management of government."[2] The pressure system, by this definition was narrowly focused both in membership and goals. Lobbyists worked largely on the margins of issues, tweaking policies in the narrow interests of their members. Politicians looked to selected lobbyists to fill them in on the details of their broad policy goals and the interests of their constituents. And the party leaders in both houses worked to put together the national coalitions needed to move the agendas of committee-generated bills. The general outlines of this rough division of labor have become blurred as the parties– Republicans in particular– have become increasingly ideological and, in effect, chosen sides in the pressure system. The perversity of this blurring was starkly illustrated in the 2017 efforts to repeal the Affordable Care Act. Under traditional rules of the game, the Republicans would have presented their repeal and replace effort as a bill referred to the relevant committees. As the committees held hearings, groups representing health insurance companies, hospitals, seniors, pharmaceutical companies and so on would have testified in public and worked to modify parts of the law. The bill would have been amended and refined as it moved through the committees of each house and through the leadership to the floor. Instead, the bill(s) were drafted in private and presented in a closed package. When the first effort failed, a second was prepared, again without the advice or arguments of the affected groups, but solely in a search for more Republican support. When that failed, there was yet a third iteration of same process. Despite the substantive differences between them, 47 Republican Senators indicated support for all three bills. What they were in effect saying was something like this:

Do you support the idea that health insurance providers should not be able to deny coverage to people with pre-existing conditions? Yes I supported legislation to do that.

Do you support legislation that allows health insurance providers to deny coverage to people with pre-existing conditions? Yes, I supported legislation to do that.

Do you support leaving the question of pre-existing conditions to the states? Yes I supported that. The same bizarre story was essentially repeated in the House.

Each of the 2017 health care bills was, to be sure, complicated, and each contained issues other than coverage for people with pre-existing conditions. In the "normal" course of the legislative process, these complications would have been worked out through a series of compromises in which the rules on this part of the health care act would have been balanced against each other. Here, however, all that mattered was the majority party's promise to repeal and replace Obamacare. With what? No matter. How? No matter. With who's council and advice? No matter. In the brave new world of a new political order, symbols displace substance, campaign politics replace legislative processes, and ideology trumps rationality. This is a world, not of Aristotelean logic but of Orwellian double- (or triple-) speak that threatens to subvert some of the most basic principles of our constitutional system. And then, as if compound the felony, the tax reform bill was crafted in much the same behind-the-curtains, top-down fashion.

The old system was not without serious flaws. What is often called "Madisonian pluralism," from James Madison's brilliant defense of group politics in the *Federalist Papers,* was never as balanced a system of give-and-take as it was cracked up to be. Despite the arguments of more modern group theorists that pluralism could almost divinely produce an equitable balance of power, the fact was and is that, as Schattschneider argued many years ago, the heavenly choir sings with an upper-class bias.[3] While some of the work of interest groups took place behind closed doors and– particularly since the Supreme Court opened the doors to virtually unlimited and untraceable campaign contributions– much of the Washington work of lobbyists remained relatively transparent. With bills like the repeal and replace health program and the 2017 tax "reform" proposals there is no such transparency, and– perhaps more importantly– none of the expert if biased public vetting of the opinions of affected groups.

The original Affordable Care Act, as we have noted, was not a model of transparency and due process; but the contrast with "repeal and replace" is in some ways exemplary of two different models of the how interest group politics works. In the original fight, the organized forces fighting over health care issues in Washington were diverse and to a considerable degree balanced. Major players included health insurance companies, the American Medical Association and groups representing practitioners of various medical specialties, labor unions, state governments, hospitals, groups advocating for particular health threats such as cancer, large employers and the American Association of Retired People. The conflicts between and among them are informatively transparent. To be sure, there were two major flaws in the representational profile of the groups struggle: the big pharmaceutical companies, on the one hand, were clearly major players and the general public generally under-represented.

But contrast this with "repeal and replace." Since the House and Senate bills were drafted (and revised) in secret one-party meetings, we have no tangible information on what interest groups were involved. The circumstantial evidence, however, strongly suggests that the pharmaceutical companies were alone among the usual groups involved in consideration of health care issues. They were alone among the usual players in health care politics who did not react with surprise and opposition to the bills as they emerged; and unlike other groups, their campaign contributions to members of the drafting teams increased dramatically. Most importantly, despite an angry public, presidential rhetoric, and numerous, sometimes bi-partisan efforts in Congress to control drug prices, none of these were reflected in any of the repeal and replace bills.[4] Similarly, in the 2017 tax cut, the details took back seat to the symbolic importance simply of passing a bill. When Senate Majority leader Mitch McConnell was asked what he supported in the bill, he reportedly answered that he supported "fifty votes." "He wanted a victory. He was open to what that looked like."[5] As with Repeal and Replace there were no public hearings and the bill was drafted almost entirely by senior staff. There was one public mark-up session in which virtually all proposed amendments were rejected on party-line votes.

This kind of off-stage, partisan lobbying is what Madison feared. Trying to check direct democracy– the kind recently called populism– the founders constructed a system that emphasized checks and balances, numerous access points, and institutional arrangements that made bargaining and compromise essential. When interest groups know that their arguments will be weighed against others, they make their best case. A starting point is to build pluralism into campaign 2020. To put people back into politics is to put associations back as well, to back candidates who cultivate expertise instead of taking orders from large donors or party leaders. Restoring viable pluralism and rationality in politics depends in part on electing representatives who have a genuine interest in issues and whose base of support is at the grassroots. "A party system consisting entirely of ideologically defined networks of activists and elites and devoid of real mass organizations" cannot do this.[6] What Suzanne Mettler describes as a growing "government-citizen disconnect" derives in large part from this organizational vacuum.

> If these institutions are functioning well, they can help citizens interpret their experiences of policies, 'connecting the dots' to understand the role that government plays in their lives. Alternatively, these institutions may lose such capacity if they grow weaker– as have labor unions over the past four decades, for example. Some groups may emerge, furthermore, that purposefully obfuscate the salutary role that government plays in American's lives and aim to transform the image of government into a hostile entity. These latter developments have characterized the past several decades of American political development.[7]

## The Changing Scope and Bias of the Pressure System

As with electoral politics, the key to balancing the upper class bias of the pressure system is to put people back into pressure politics. This is particularly important for liberals who, with the decline of organized labor, are losing their strongest voice. Using the leverage given them by the changing campaign finance rules, a small group of very wealthy donors have become so crucial to congressional Republicans that they virtually control Republican policy. Democrats are moving in that direction. Large independent political action committees are now generally estimated to spend more money anonymously on campaigns than all regulated donors combined. Even among the financial supporters of both parties that can be identified, almost half of the money donated comes from a tiny handful of very large donors who collectively account for as much as two-thirds of all campaign funds. To the extent that Big Pharma was the only health interest in the room when repeal and replace was being put together, so it appears were the House and Senate tax "reforms" crafted with only a small slice of the business community in the room. Interestingly, the number of organized groups with advocacy offices in Washington, which had been growing for more than a century, has actually declined by more than thirty percent since 2006.[8] As popular as it is for politicians to rail against "special interests," they are doing so at a time when the visible groups in Washington are fading from power. Few Washington lobbyists face imminent unemployment, but with Republicans in power they are, ironically, increasingly marginal to a legislative process that is increasingly dominated by the most affluent of all special interests that work, not through the partially open arena of the pressure system, but by covertly capturing the congressional leadership. Why spend money on a Washington office working on the details of policy and working to persuade fifty-one Senators to take your side when the Majority Leader controls the agenda? As many as a third of the Republican members of the House, my Washington friends tell me, have no one on their staff who can talk about policy issues. The universe of policy voices is rapidly shrinking. One small but significant indicator: "as power shifted from committee leaders to party leaders, committees did significantly less work. In 1979-80, House committees held 7,033 meetings. By 1999-2000, committees held only 3,374 meetings."[9] To extend Schattschneider's oft-quoted metaphor, the heavenly chorus still sings with in upper-class bias, but it performs increasingly in private parlors rather than public concerts.

A recent book by Matt Grossman and David Hopkins argues that the nature of the two parties is increasingly asymmetric. "While the Democratic Party is fundamentally a group coalition, the Republican Party can be most accurately characterized as the vehicle of an ideological movement."[10] The core Republican principle favoring less government, particularly at the national level, resonates well with voters, but the specific policy proposals that flow from it do not. Indeed Republican success at the polls has derived almost entirely from perceptions of what they are against. While Democrats are often criticized for not having a unifying ideology, their positions on specific issues tend to have broad popular support. It makes sense, in this context, to play to strength rather than weakness, to hit the Republicans not with a losing appeal for big government (as it would be portrayed), but with calls for defending and expanding specific programs already having widespread approval such as Medicare, renewable energy, bank regulation, public education, and so on.

Effective advocacy on these and other issues runs along two tracks. In the short run, there are always openings for influence on narrow issues: seeking a legislator's help in finding sources of funding for a local library, protesting the proposed route of a pipeline, making sure that the research budget for health continues to include a specific rare disease. On larger issues, the key is to deconstruct the Republican ideology, to show how cuts and changes in programs affect real people. What I call agitation can abet this process in two ways: on the one hand– as was shown in the failed attempts to repeal and replace Obamacare– through the hundreds of thousands of people who turned out to focus on the real effects of specific aspects of the bills on ordinary people; and, on the other hand, through the effects of these efforts on consolidating opposition forces and changing the agenda of political discourse. This is what the Democratic club efforts on the War in Viet Nam and gay rights, described earlier in this chapter, sought to do: they didn't end the war, they didn't end discrimination; they did change the terms of discourse. As Schattschneider argued "the definition of alternatives is the supreme instrument of power. . . He who determines what politics is about runs the country, because the definition of alternatives is the choice of conflicts, and the choice of conflicts allocates power."[11] Read that again, because it gets to the essence of what I am trying to say about the two tracks of advocacy. Lobbying, in the narrow sense of trying to change public policy, is effective largely on the margins of major issues, usually quite specialized in its objectives, and aimed directly at office holders rather than voters. Agitation is not about the specifics of policy. If it is aimed at an office holder, it targets him or her as a symbol: its real target is public opinion. What this means, in practical terms, is that the techniques and tactics that work for agitators are not particularly useful for lobbyists and vice versa. What about lobbying?

## Effective Lobbying

As a newly-minted PhD in 1963 I found myself in the heady position of Legislative Assistant to the junior senator from Indiana, Birch Bayh. One of my jobs was to prepare a daily memo briefly summarizing the bills likely to come to the floor, together with the positions of major interest groups and my own recommendation. Early in my new job there was a bill from a Senator from Wisconsin changing the system for milk marketing quotas. What I knew about milk was that it came from cows. I read the bill and the committee report and, quite frankly, couldn't figure it out. The Agriculture Committee person I talked with was not much help, and the Farmer's Union lobbyist I called was busy. The Senator, as a Democrat, generally preferred the advice of the Farmer's Union to the more conservative Farm Bureau, but Herb Harris of the Bureau was in my office an hour after I called. His lucid explanation of the bill virtually wrote my memo, but his bottom line was a surprise. We're for this bill, he said, but it's not good for Indiana. Your guy should vote against it, and he explained why.

Mr. Harris did not help the Bureau's cause on that bill, but he became my go-to guy on agricultural issues. And this tells you three very important things about lobbying. First, most members of Congress and their staff people don't think of lobbying as "pressure." Interest groups provide an important service for politicians with an interest in good public policy. My guess is that as many of the contacts between politicians and their staff people, on the one hand, and lobbyists on the other, are initiated by the former. Second, the prime currency of interest group effectiveness is trust. Inside the beltway nothing is more important than credibility, or as one congressman bluntly puts it: "Snow is for the folks, it don't fly here." Third, lobbying, by and large, is organizational, on-going and informed. Citizen lobbyists are triply disadvantaged: lacking in-depth knowledge they have relatively little expertise to provide; lacking a history of relations, it is difficult for them to acquire trust; and lacking an ongoing organizational presence, they are hard to find. But they also have some significant, if too-seldom tapped strengths.

Let us note from the outset that citizen lobbyists, unlike many professionals, seldom have either the financial or research resources that enable professionals to work across district lines. Letters and phone calls from non-constituents are seldom counted or taken seriously. And the angrier they are, the less their credibility. It makes sense, unless she's thinking of moving to Florida or running for President, why should a Senator from Iowa care about a ranting letter from the sunshine state? A young lawyer, hired by a very conservative Senator was given– as one of his first chores– the task of answering a pile of letters from all over the country dealing with questions for which the office had no stock answers. After working through most of them, he was left with a small pile accusing the Senator of everything but mass murder. "How do I respond to these?" he asked. "Give them a noncommittal answer," the Senator replied. "Well, I figured that, but what specifically should I say?" "Tell them to go fuck themselves," the Senator replied. Some staffers still use the phrase "give them a noncommittal answer" as a euphemism for what they really mean.

But citizen lobbyists, working in their own districts have some very real advantages. Most importantly, they know their districts and their local concerns; they don't get noncommittal answers when they write. Unlike Herb Harris, moreover, many local citizen lobbyists don't have to earn their legislator's trust: they already have it, as friends, neighbors and, most importantly, as parts of their winning campaigns. "Each member of Congress," Richard Fenno argues, "perceives four concentric constituencies: geographic, reelection, primary and personal."[12] Only a small number of campaign volunteers, if any, work their way into the innermost of these circles, the family members and oldest friends with whom they have both political and emotional connections; but the primary circle, sometimes defined as "the ones each congressman believes would provide his last line of electoral defense in a primary contest"[13] is often comprised largely of volunteers. These are the people Birch Bayh called the "stand up sons-of-a-bitches," those who when you need to get a mailing right away mutter "son-of-a-bitch" and stand up to get it done. When these people visited in Washington, they had as much access as his largest contributors. Indeed research suggests that what some academics call "social lobbying," the ability to talk to members in informal settings is particularly effective.

Those in what Fenno calls the reelection circle, may not have privileged access, but the door is usually open. What about active Democrats represented by Republicans (and vice versa)? By and large, they get noncommittal answers, especially when the numbers of letters, phone calls, e-mails and demonstrators are relatively small. These cross-party lobbying efforts can have an impact, however, in the following kinds of ways. It can matter when there are large numbers of people, not all of them known partisans, who seem generally concerned about the negative effects of proposed legislation. This occurred in 2017 in many districts on repeal and replace health care bills where the usual suspects were joined by people not known to be partisans but sincerely concerned about the personal impact of the bills on their lives. When doctors, seniors, people with pre-existing conditions, and so on joined the demonstrations, it made a difference. While few congressional minds were changed, the impact on district opinion was sometimes significant, particularly in districts where representatives openly avoided or dismissed public dialogue. Group efforts on issues of this kind are where advocacy moves from lobbying to agitation and where they can also morph into recruitment opportunities for future electoral activity.

A second kind of effective lobbying across party lines works for people with specific and particular experience or expertise. A thoughtful letter, especially on an arcane subject, that details a businessperson's experience with a costly but unnecessary regulation, a consumer's experience with an unregulated type of fraud, a former diplomat's tale of mistaken American policies in another country, these are grist for the congressional mill. Even in today' hyper-partisan era, a bipartisan bill to relieve smaller banks from some of the restrictions imposed by Dodd-Franks made it through. On narrow issues such as this, the old-fashioned Madisonian system still works. So too, unfortunately, does an equally effective commodity, money– big money that is– cross district lines. The basic rule of thumb, however, is that politicians look first to their districts, to individuals and groups from inside it, to national organizations that have substantial numbers of members in the district, and to those who can fund their campaigns. Writing letters to those outside of you district can satisfy the soul and perhaps sustain a volunteer base, but in terms of influencing policy is essentially a waste of time. Demonstrating in front of a member's office may have an impact on public opinion but is unlikely to change votes.

## Legislative Intelligence

When it does come to lobbying, here are the things legislators, at least those who have some independence from party leaders, want to know: what is the problem seeking solution, what can be done by whom, who will it hurt or help, and how will it play in a future campaign? Members of Congress are overwhelmed with data: literally dozens of reports are generated every week by government agencies, private foundations, state governments, interest groups, journalists and academics, many of them relevant to the work the legislature. Looking at the figures pieced together in one of the leading texts on interest groups in American politics, it can be calculated that the average member of Congress receives roughly 370,000 letter, e-mails, telephone calls and faxes every year, more than a thousand a day.[14] What legislators need are methods of refining, winnowing and making political sense of this data overload. To do this,

> Outside of the areas in which he himself has special knowledge and interest, the legislator needs sources of information which can combine, in one neat package, an evaluation of a program's significance, popularity, and relationship to other negotiable issues. The most economical form in which such information can be packaged is that which contains the least data. The best information that he [or she] can have on some issues is a reliable directive to vote yes or no.[15]

The tricky part of this is the word *reliable*. And this is where the citizen lobbyist is particularly advantaged (or disadvantaged, as the case may be) by the simple fact of being a known commodity, known, if not personally, at least by reputation. The better you know your representative and, more importantly, the better he or she knows you, the more probable your access.

> Legislators are not beginning with a blank slate. All have a sense of who their consistent supporters are, who are consistent opponents and who occupy the spaces in between. . . . Most legislators play a conservative game and follow the preferences of their most consistent supporters rather than those of their past opponents.[16]

They play to their base, and pay special attention to those who are known commodities. In many cases, this gives local activists a good part of the credibility that every lobbyist seeks.

106

Credibility is based on more than just familiarity. Above all it depends on having useful information in digested form, intelligence, as I like to call it, as opposed to information. It combines processed and evaluated technical information with an understanding of local politics and economic conditions. It includes realism, not asking for something that is politically or fiscally impossible– when you ask that you go from providing help to being a pain. It may often include an honest portrayal of opposing arguments, because "good information is important not just for arguing within Congress but also for justifying one's position to constituents." As Levine continues, "As unquestionable as is the congressional thirst for good information, the distaste for bad information is even more pronounced."[17] Building trust begins, at a minimum, with building competence. There is no doubt that a well-organized, well-financed Washington or state lobbying office is tremendously advantaged in both its ability to develop a bank of expert knowledge for officeholders to draw upon, and a continuing availability in the capitol.

In the best case scenario, these lobbying offices are able to mobilize large numbers of members, customers, clients and friends to contact their legislators. The idea is that if, say, all the automobile dealers in a legislator's district write to support a specific bill, their lobbyist is more likely to be able to find a receptive audience when he or she comes to make the case. Many state legislatures have formal advocacy days, organized by professional lobbyists, where hundreds of gun owners, college students and faculty, senior citizens, hikers, small business owners and union members roam the halls visiting their local State Senators and Assembly members to, in effect, soften them up for a more detailed and professional presentation .

For political activists, the point of grassroots campaigns goes beyond such short-term goals. First, in terms of the case made in this book for putting people back in politics, it is part of a longer range strategy to build a movement. Just as professional campaign managers play an important role in elections, but are more effective when joined with citizen activists, so are professional lobbyists strengthened by their links to constituents. Second, rallying around issues is an effective vehicle for sustaining organizations between elections and forging new alliances. And finally there are (fortunately) voters who really do care about issues and who want to be represented by legislators who do. So even if many (if not most) Republican incumbents play follow the leader and have little use for expert opinion, there are good reasons to establish advocacy groups, to engage in issues research, and at least go through the motions of lobbying.

Grassroots lobbying is only as effective as its follow-up. A California Congressman, Clem Miller, once compared two groups– walnut growers and chicken farmers– who had lobbying days in Washington. The walnut growers, though far less numerous than the poultry people, got pretty much what they wanted, the chicken farmers nothing. The difference was that the walnut group hired a lobbyist to follow up on their visit. He or she sent a follow-up letter to each of the legislators the farmers had visited and then visited their offices with a specific plan of action. The good will generated by the chicken farmers, conversely, faded away as they went home leaving it up to the Congresswomen to initiate a policy. No matter how good the cause, getting legislators to pay attention to your issue is not easy: the chicken farmers lost not because of active opposition but because the Congressmen they contacted had more pressing concerns. Most legislators pretty much know how they are going to vote on most issues: what is easier and more important to influence is what they do with their time. It helps, of course, to have a paid professional to do this follow up work; but there is no reason that dedicated volunteers, in lobbying as in campaigns cannot shoulder much of the burden.

## People Power

The road back toward a more rational, reasoned and compassionate polity is long. It is made all the more difficult by a widespread and growing mistrust of government, science and expertise in general. Fueled munificently by a handful of ideological fanatics hiding behind the destruction of campaign finance regulations, the radical rich are well on the way to destroying democracy as we know it. We can write checks to decent candidates and if enough of us do, we might be able partially to match the tens of millions given each year by a large network of big donors, but the gap is huge.[18] We are learning, moreover, that in an ideological battle between those favoring the abstraction of more government rather than less, Democrats lose. Democrats win when they shift attention to concrete issues and the real problems of real people. They can win too, as I have argued, when they put people back into politics shifting the locus of campaigns from wholesale to retail and putting a human face on the message. And there is more. If and when Democrats put these ideas into practice (and maybe even before then) some Republicans– equally disgusted with ideologically divisive and pay to play politics– may themselves look to grassroots organizing and bring the G.O.P. back to its roots.

In the model campaign I have tried to describe here, post-modern volunteer politics and lobbying– the party system and the pressure system, if you well– blend almost seamlessly. When activists visit their friends and neighbors, registering voters, discussing issues and recording their concerns, they build data bases that combine geographic and issue constituencies. When the campaign has a thorough mapping of the district, and in particular as an ongoing organization builds a data set from one year to the next, it will have also built issue networks. It will, in essence, have networks of voters with common interests in environmental issues, immigration, civil rights, health care and so on that can be mobilized for advocacy and lobbying. And it will be able, through these networks, to convey the ideas of voters to their elected officials.

The radical labor organizer Joe Hill asked on his death bed that his followers "don't mourn for me, organize." We must do the same. Whether the task is campaigns and elections, agitation or lobbying, organization is what makes it work in the long run. And it will be a long run. No matter how well progressive forces do in the 2020 elections, the wahoos will still have the power to stop or delay major initiatives. And to roll back the gerrymanders, restrictions on voting rights and campaign finance rules that so distort majority rule will take years. And it may be years beyond that before the American people have confidence enough in themselves to restore their faith in democratic government. John F. Kennedy was fond of the Chinese proverb that the longest journey begins with a single step. If 2018 was that first step, this is time for the second.

# Endnotes

1   Gary W. Cox and Matthew D. McCubbin, Setting the Agenda: Responsible Government in the U. S. House of Representatives (New York: Cambridge University Press, 2003).

2   V. O. Key, Politics, Parties, and Pressure Groups (New York: Alfred A. Knopf, 4th ed., 1998), 23.

3   E. E. Schattschneider, The Semisovereign People: A Realist's View of Democracy in America (New York: Holt, Rinehart and Winston, 1960). See also Lee Drutman, The Business of America is Lobbying: How Corporations Became Politicized and Politics Became More Corporate (New York: Oxford University Press, 2015).

4   Jay Hancock, "Big Pharma Can't Lose," The New York Times, September 24, 2017, F7.

5   Jake Sherman and Anna Palmer, The Hill to Die On: The Battle for Congress and the Future of Trump's America (New York: Crown, 2019), 167.

6   Sam Rosenfeld, The Polarizers: Postwar Architects of Our Partisan Era (Chicago: University of Chicago Press, 2018), 284.

7   Suzanne Mettler, The Government-Citizen Disconnect ((New York: Russell Sage Foundation, 2018), 145.

8   The Center for Responsive Politics has been tracking these numbers for twenty years. Because they count only those who have actually registered under the law, their figures are generally thought to be lower than the number of groups that occasionally contact government officials.

9   Kathryn Pearson, "The Constitution and Congressional Leadership," in William F. Connelly, Jr., John J. Pitney, Jr, and Gary J. Schmitt, Is Congress Broken: The Virtues and Defects of Partisanship and Gridlock (Washington: The Brookings Institution, 2017), 169.

10  Matt Grossman and David A. Hopkins, Asymmetric Politics: Ideological Republicans and Group Interest Democrats (New York: Oxford University Press, 2016), 3.

11  Schattschneider, 68.

12  Richard F. Fenno, Jr., Home Style: House Members in Their Districts (Boston: Little, Brown, 1978), 27.

13  Ibid. 18.

14  Anthony J. Nownes, Interest Groups in American Politics: Pressure and Power (New York: Routledge, 2nd ed., 2013), 175.

15  Edward Schneier, "The Intelligence of Congress: Information and Public-Policy Patterns," 388 Annals of the American Academy of Political and Social Science (March 1970), 18.

16  R. Douglas Arnold, The Logic of Congressional Action (New Haven: Yale University Press, 1990), 83.

17  Bertram J. Levine, The Art of Lobbying: Building Trust and Selling Policy (Washington: CQ Press, 2009), 135.

18  Jane Mayer, Dark Money: The Hidden History of the Billionaires behind the Rise of the Radical Right (New York: Doubleday, 2016).

# Appendix A: The One Hundred and One Most Marginal House Districts in 2020

| State and District | 2016 | 2018 | Presidential Margin in 2016 | Rating | Targeted |
|---|---|---|---|---|---|
| Alaska AL | R: Young 50.3<br>D: Lindbeck 36.1 | R: Young 53.3<br>D: Galvin 46.7 | R +15.2 | Likely R | |
| Arizona 1 | D: O'Halleran 50.8<br>R: Babeu 43.5 | D: O'Halleran 53.8<br>R: Rogers 46.2 | R +1.1 | Likely D | RCCC |
| Arizona 2 | R: McSally 56.7*<br>D: Heinz 43.3 | D: Kirkpatrick 54.7<br>R: Peterson 45.3 | D +4.9 | Likely D | RCCC |
| Arizona 6 | R: Schweikert 62.1<br>D: Williamson 37.9 | R: Schweikert 55.2<br>D: Malik 44.8 | R +10 | Likely R | DCCC |
| Arkansas 2 | R: Hill 58.3<br>D: Curry 36.8 | R: Hill 52.1<br>D: Tucker 45.8 | R +11 | Likely R | |
| California 1 | R: Lamalfa 59.1<br>D: Reed 40.9 | R: Lamalfa 54.9<br>D: Denney 45.1 | R +10 | Likely R | |
| California 4 | R: McClintock 62.7<br>D: Derlet 37.3 | R: McClintock 54.1<br>D: Morse 45.9 | R +14 | Likely R | |
| California 7 | D: Bera 51.2<br>R: Jones 48.8 | D: Bera 55.0<br>R: Grant 45.0 | D +11.4 | Likely D | |
| California 10 | R: Denham 51.7<br>D: Eggman | D: Harder 52.3<br>R: Denham 47.7 | D +3.0 | Leans D | RCCC |

| California 21 | R: Valadao 56.7<br>D: Huerta 43.3 | D: Cox 50.4<br>R: Valadao 49.6 | R +25.8 | Leans D | RCCC |
|---|---|---|---|---|---|
| California 22 | R: Nunes 67.6<br>D: Campos 32.4 | R: Nunes 52.7<br>D: Janz 47.3 | R +10 | Likely R | DCCC |
| California 25 | R: Knight 53.1<br>D: Caforio 46.9 | D: Hill 54.4**<br>R: Knight 45.6 | D +6.7 | Leans D | RCCC |
| California 39 | R: Royce 57.2*<br>D: Murdock 42.8 | D: Cisneros 51.6<br>R: Kim 48.4 | D +8.6 | Leans D | RCCC |
| California 45 | R: Walters 58.6<br>D: Varasteh 51.4 | D: Porter 52.0<br>R: Walters 47.9 | D +5.4 | Likely D | RCCC |
| California 48 | R: Rohrabacher 58.3<br>D: Savary 41.7 | D: Rouda 53.6<br>R: Rohrabacher 46.4 | D +1.7 | Leans D | |
| California 50 | R: Hunter 63.5<br>D: Malloy 36.5 | R: Hunter 51.7**<br>D: Campa-Najjar 48.3 | R +15 | Leans R | DCCC |
| Colorado 3 | R: Tipton 54.6<br>D: Schwartz 40.4 | R: Tipton 51.5<br>D: Bush 43.6 | R +12 | Likely R | DCCC |
| Colorado 6 | R: Coffman 50.9<br>D: Carroll 42.6 | D: Crow 54.1<br>R: Coffman 42.9 | D +8.9 | Likely D | RCCC |
| Florida 15 | R: Ross 57.5<br>D: Lange 42.5 | R: Spano 53.0<br>D: Carlson 47.0 | R +10 | Likely R | DCCC |
| Florida 16 | R: Buchanan 59.8<br>D: Schneider 40.2 | R: Buchanan 54.6<br>D: Shapiro 45.4 | R +11 | Likely R | DCCC |
| Florida 18 | R: Mast 53.6<br>D: Perkins 43.1 | R: Mast 54.3<br>D: Baer 45.7 | R +9.2 | Likely R | DCCC |
| Florida 26 | R: Curbelo 53.0<br>D: Garcia 41.2 | D: Mucarsel-Powell 50.9<br>R: Curbelo 49.1 | R +16.3 | Likely D | RCCC |

| District | | | | | |
|---|---|---|---|---|---|
| Florida 27 | R: Ross-Lehtinen 54.9*<br>D: Fuhrman 45.1 | D: Shalala 51.8<br>R: Salazar 45.8 | R +19.6 | Likely D | RCCC |
| Georgia 6 | See note 1 | D: McBath 50.5<br>R: Handel 49.5 | R +1.5 | Leans D | RCCC |
| Georgia 7 | R: Woodall 60.4<br>D: Malik 39.6 | R: Woodall 50.1**<br>D: Bourdeax 49.9 | R +6 | Toss-up | DCCC |
| Illinois 6 | R: Roskam 59.2<br>D: Howland 40.8 | D: Kasten 53.6<br>R: Roskam 46.4 | D +7.0 | Leans D | RCCC |
| Illinois 12 | R: Bost 54.3<br>D: Baricevic 39.7 | R: Bost 51.6<br>D: Kelly 45.4 | R +14.8 | Likely R | |
| Illinois 13 | R: Davis 59.7<br>D: Wicklund 40.3 | R: Davis 50.4<br>D: Londrigan 49.6 | R +5.5 | Leans R | DCCC |
| Illinois 14 | R: Hultgren 59.3<br>D: Walz 40.7 | D: Underwood 52.5<br>R: Hultgren 47.5 | R +3.9 | Toss-up | RCCC |
| Indiana 5 | R: Brooks 61.5<br>D: Demaree 34.5 | R: Brooks 56.8**<br>D: Thornton 43.2 | R +12 | Leans R | DCCC |
| Iowa 1 | R: Blum 53.8<br>D: Vernon 46.2 | D: Finkenauer 51.0<br>R: Blum 45.9 | R +3.5 | Toss-up | RCCC |
| Iowa 2 | D: Loebsack 53.7<br>R: Peters 46.3 | D: Loebsack 54.8**<br>R: Peters 42.6 | R +4.1 | Toss-up | RCCC |
| Iowa 3 | R: Young 53.5<br>D: Mowrer 39.8 | D: Axne 49.3<br>R: Young 47.1 | R +3.5 | Toss-up | RCCC |
| Iowa 4 | R: King 61.2<br>D: Weaver 38.6 | R: King 50.3<br>D: Scholton 47.0 | R +17 | Likely R | DCCC |
| Kansas 2 | R: Jenkins 60.9*<br>D: Potter 32.5 | R: Watkins 47.6<br>D: Davis 46.8 | R +18.4 | Likely R | |

| | | | | | |
|---|---|---|---|---|---|
| Kansas 3 | R: Yoder 51.3<br>D: Sidie 40.6 | D: Davis 53.6<br>R: Yoder 43.9 | D +1.2 | Leans D | RCCC |
| Kentucky 6 | R: Barr 61.1<br>D: Kemper 38.9 | R: Barr 51.0<br>D: McGrath 47.8 | R +15.3 | Likely R | DCCC |
| Maine 2 | R: Poliquin 54.9<br>D: Cain 45.1 | D: Golden 50.6<br>R: Polquin 49.4 | R +10.3 | Toss-up | |
| Michigan 3 | R: Amash 59.5<br>D: Smith 37.5 | R: Amash 54.4<br>D: Albro 43.2 | R +10 | Toss-up | DCCC |
| Michigan 6 | R: Upton 58.6<br>D: Clements 36.5 | R: Upton 50.2<br>D: Longjohn 45.7 | R +8 | Likely R | DCCC |
| Michigan 7 | R: Walberg 55.1<br>D: Driskell 40.0 | R: Walberg 53.8<br>D: Driskell 46.2 | R + 10 | Likely R | |
| Michigan 8 | R: Bishop 56.0<br>D: Shkreli 39.2 | D: Slotkin 50.5<br>R: Bishop 46.8 | R +6.7 | Leans D | RCCC |
| Michigan 11 | R: Trott 52.9*<br>D: Kumar 40.2 | D: Stevens 51.8<br>R: Epstein 45.2 | R +4.44 | Leans D | RCCC |
| Minnesota 1 | D: Walz 50.4*<br>R: Hagedorn 49.6 | R: Hagedorn 50.2<br>D: Feehan 49.7 | R +14.9 | Likely R | DCCC |
| Minnesota 2 | R: Lewis 47.2<br>D: Craig 45.2 | D: Craig 52.7<br>R: Lewis 47.2 | R +1.2 | Leans D | RCCC |
| Minnesota 3 | R: Paulsen 56.9<br>D: Bonoff 43.1 | D: Phillips 55.6<br>R: Paulsen 44.2 | R +9.4 | Likely D | RCCC |
| Minnesota 7 | D: Peterson 52.5<br>R: Hughes 47.5 | D: Peterson 52.1<br>R: Hughes 47.8 | R + 30.8 | Toss-up | RCCC |
| Minnesota 8 | D: Nolan 50.3*<br>R: Mills 49.7 | R: Stauber 50.7<br>D: Radinovich 45.2 | D +7.8 | Likely R | |

116

| Missouri 2 | R: Wagner 58.6 | R: Wagner 51.2 | R +11 | Leans R | DCCC |
|---|---|---|---|---|---|
| | D: Otto 37.7 | D: VanOstran 47.2 | | | |
| Montana at large | See note 2 | R: Gianforte 50.9** | R +20.6 | Likely R | DCCC |
| | | D: Williams 46.2 | | | |
| Nebraska 2 | R: Bacon 49.4 | R: Bacon 51.0 | R +2.2 | Leans R | DCCC |
| | D: Ashford 47.3 | D: Eastman 49.0 | | | |
| Nevada 3 | D: Rosen 47.2* | D: Lee 51.9 | R +1.0 | Leans D | |
| | R: Tarkanian 46.0 | R: Tarkanian 42.8 | | | |
| Nevada 4 | D: Kilhuen 48.5* | D: Horsford 51.9 | D +4.9 | Likely D | |
| | R: Hardy 44.5 | R: Hardy 43.8 | | | |
| New Hampshire 1 | D: Shea-Porter 44.2* | D: Pappas 53.6 | R +1.6 | Leans D | RCCC |
| | R: Guinta 42.9 | R: Edwards 45.0 | | | |
| New Jersey 2 | R: LoBiondi 59.4* | D: Van Drew 52.9 | R +4.6 | Leans D | RCCC |
| | D: Cole 37.1 | R: Grossman 45.2 | | | |
| New Jersey 3 | R: MacArthur 59.5 | D: Kim 50.0 | R +6.6 | Toss-up | RCCC |
| | D: LaVergne 38.6 | R: MacArthur 48.7 | | | |
| New Jersey 7 | R: Lance 54.2 | D: Malinowski 51.7 | D +1.1 | Leans D | RCCC |
| | D: Jacob 43.0 | R: Lance 46.7 | | | |
| New Jersey 11 | R: Frelinghuysen 58.2* | D: Sherrill 56.8 | R +.9 | Likely D | RCCC |
| | D: Wenzel 38.7 | R: Webber 42.1 | | | |
| New Mexico 2 | R: Pearce 62.7* | D: Small 50.9 | R +10.2 | Toss-up | RCCC |
| | D: Soules 37.3 | R: Herrell 49.1 | | | |
| New York 1 | R: Zeldin 59.0 | R: Zeldin 51.5 | R +12.3 | Likely R | DCCC |
| | D: Throne-Holst 41.0 | D: Gershon 47.4 | | | |
| New York 2 | R: King 62.1 | R: King 53.1** | R +9 | Leans R | DCCC |
| | D: Gregory 37.9 | D: Shirley 46.9 | | | |

| District | | | | | |
|---|---|---|---|---|---|
| New York 11 | R: Donovan 62.2<br>D: Reichard 36.1 | D: Rose 53.0<br>R: Donovan 46.6 | R +9.8 | Toss-up | RCCC |
| New York 18 | D: Maloney 55.6<br>R: Oliva 44.4 | D: Maloney 55.5<br>R: O'Donnell 44.5 | R +1.9 | Likely D | RCCC |
| New York 19 | R: Faso 54.7<br>D: Teachout 45.3 | D: Delgado 51.4<br>R: Faso 46.2 | R +6.8 | Toss-up | RCCC |
| New York 21 | R: Stefanik 65.3<br>D: Derrick 30.2 | R: Stefanik 56.1<br>D: Cobb 42.4 | R +14 | Likely R | |
| New York 22 | R: Tenney 47.2<br>D: Myers 40.4 | D: Brindisi 50.9<br>R: Tenney 49.1 | R +15.5 | Toss-up | RCCC |
| New York 24 | R: Katco 61.0<br>D: Deacon 39.0 | R: Katko 52.6<br>D: Balter 47.4 | D +3.6 | Likely R | DCCC |
| New York 27 | R: Collins 67.2<br>D: Kastenbaum 32.8 | R: Collins 49.1**<br>D: McMurray 48.8 | R +24 | Likely R | DCCC |
| North Carolina 2 | R: Holding 56.7<br>D: McNiel 43.3 | R: Holding 51.3<br>D: Coleman 45.8 | R +9.6 | Leans R | DCCC |
| North Carolina 9 | R: Pittinger 58.3<br>D: Cano 41.7 | R: Harris 49.3<br>D: McCready 48.9 | R +11.6 | Likely R | DCCC |
| North Carolina 13 | R: Budd 56.1<br>D: Davis 43.9 | R: Budd 51.6<br>D: Manning 45.5 | R +9.4 | Likely R | DCCC |
| Ohio 1 | R: Chabot 59.6<br>D: Young 50.4 | R: Chabot 51.3<br>D: Pureval 46.9 | R +6.6 | Leans R | DCCC |
| Ohio 12 | R: Tiberi 66.6*<br>D: Albertson 29.8 | R: Balderson 51.4<br>D: O'Conner 47.2 | R +11.3 | Likely R | DCCC |
| Oklahoma 5 | R: Russell 57.1<br>D: McCaffrey 36.8 | D: Horn 50.7<br>R: Russell 49.3 | R +13 | Toss-up | RCCC |

| District | | | | | |
|---|---|---|---|---|---|
| Pennsylvania 1 | R: Fitzpatrick 54.4<br>D: Santasiero 45.6 | R: Fitzpatrick 51.3<br>D: Wallace 48.7 | D +4 | Leans R | DCCC |
| Pennsylvania 6 | R: Costello 57.3<br>D: Parrish 42.7 | R: Costello 56.3<br>D: Trivedi 43.7 | D +.6 | Leans D | |
| Pennsylvania 7 | R: Meehan 59.7*<br>D: Balchunis 40.3 | D: Wild 53.5<br>R: Nothstein 43.5 | D +2.3 | Likely D | RCCC |
| Pennsylvania 8 | D: Cartwright 53.8<br>R: Connolly 46.2 | D: Cartwright 54.6<br>R: Chin 45.4 | D +.2 | Leans D | RCCC |
| Pennsylvania 10 | R: Perry 66.1<br>D: Burkholder 33.9 | R: Perry 51.3<br>D: Scott 48.7 | R +22 | Leans R | DCCC |
| Pennsylvania 11 | R: Smucker 53.9<br>D: Hartman 42.7 | R: Smucker 53.9<br>D: DiNicola 47.3 | R +6.8 | Likely R | |
| Pennsylvania 16 | R: Kelly 100.0<br>Unopposed | R: Kelly 51.6<br>D: DiNicola 47.3 | R +19.9 | Likely R | DCCC |
| Pennsylvania 17 | See Note 3 | D: Lamb 56.3<br>R: Rothfus 43.7 | | Likely D | RCCC |
| South Carolina 1 | R: Sanford 58.6*<br>D: Cherry 36.8 | D: Cunningham 50.6<br>R: Arrington 49.2 | R +13 | Toss-up | RCCC |
| Texas 2 | R: Poe 60.6<br>D: Bryan 36.0 | R: Crenshaw 52.8<br>D: Litton 45.6 | R +9 | Likely R | |
| Texas 6 | R: Barton 58.3*<br>D: Woolridge 39.0 | R: Wright 53.1<br>D: Sanchez 45.4 | R +12 | Likely R | |
| Texas 7 | R: Culberson 56.2<br>D: Cargas 43.8 | D: Fletcher 52.5<br>R: Culberson 47.5 | D +1.4 | Leans D | RCCC |
| Texas 10 | R: McCaul 57.3<br>D: Cadien 38.4 | R: McCaul 51.1<br>D: Siegel 46.8 | R +9 | Leans R | DCCC |

| Texas 21 | R: Smith 57.0 / D: Wakely 36.5 | R: Roy 50.2 / D: Kopser 47.6 | R +10 | Leans R | DCCC |
| Texas 22 | R: Olson 59.2 / D: Gibson 40.5 | R: Olson 51.4** / D: Kulkami 46.5 | R +8 | Leans R | DCCC |
| Texas 23 | R: Hurd 48.5 / D: Gallego 46.8 | R: Hurd 49.2** / D: Jones 48.7 | D +3.4 | Leans D | DCCC |
| Texas 24 | R: Marchant 56.2 / D: McDowell 39.3 | R: Marchant 50.6** / D: McDowell 47.7 | R +6 | Toss-up | DCCC |
| Texas 25 | R: Williams 58.4 / D: Thomas 37.7 | R: Williams 53.5 / D: Oliver 44.8 | R +15 | Likely R | |
| Texas 31 | R: Carter 58.4 / D: Clark 36.5 | R: Carter 50.6 / D: Hegar 47.7 | R +13 | Leans R | DCCC |
| Texas 32 | R: Sessions 71.1 / L: Stuard 19.0 | D: Allred 52.3 / R: Sessions 45.8 | D +1.9 | Leans D | RNCC |
| Utah 4 | R: Love 53.5 / D: Owens 41.7 | D: McAdams 50.1 / R: Love 49.9 | R +6.7 | Toss-up | RCCC |
| Virginia 2 | R: Taylor 61.7 / D: Brown 38.3 | D: Luria 51.1 / R: Taylor 48.8 | R +3.4 | Leans D | RCCC |
| Virginia 5 | R: Garrett 58.3 / D: Dittmar 41.7 | R: Riggleman 53.3 / D: Cockburn 46.7 | R +11.1 | Likely R | DCCC |
| Virginia 7 | R: Brat 57.5 / D: Bedell 42.2 | D: Spanberger 50.3 / R: Brat 48.4 | R +6.5 | Leans D | RCCC |
| Washington 3 | R: Beutler 62.0 / D: Moeller 38.0 | R: Beutler 52.7 / D: Long 47.3 | R +4 | Likely R | |

| Washington 8 | R: Reichert 60.0* | D: Schreier 52.4 | D +3.0 | Likely D | RCCC |
|---|---|---|---|---|---|
| | D: Ventrella 40.0 | R: Rossi 47.6 | | | |
| Wisconsin 1 | R: Ryan 65.0 | R: Steil 54.6 | R +10 | Likely D | |
| | D: Solen 30.2 | D: Bryce 42.3 | | | |

*Indicates an incumbent who retired in 2018.

**Indicates an incumbent who is not running for re-election in 2020

Note 1: Georgia's 6th District became vacant when the incumbent Republican resigned. A special election to fill the vacancy in this normally safe-Republican district saw newcomer Jon Ossoff come within fewer than 10,000 votes of a major upset. The new incumbent, Congresswoman Karen Handel won the seat for a full two year time in 2018.

Note 2: This is another case of a special election in a normally Republican district that came out closer than expected. Republican Greg Gianforte, who gained 50% of the vote compared to Rob Quist's 44.4%, won a full two year term in 2018.

Note 3: Between the 2016 and 2018 elections, Pennsylvania was redistricted by court order. Although none of the 2018 districts are strictly comparable to their predecessors, the new 17th is particularly different from its predecessor.
**Sources and Key:** Throughout recent years a number of organizations have tracked the campaigns for the House of Representatives rating them on a five-point scale of likely outcomes. Although they use different labels and slightly different calculations, districts are generally characterized as either "safe" for one party or the other, "likely" Republican or Democratic, "leaning," or too close to call ("toss up"). This table presents the major party results of the 2016 and 2018 House elections together with the average rankings for 2020 of the Cook Report, Inside Elections and Larry Sabato's Crystal Ball, plus frequent analyses reported in Politico and the New York Times. The eighty-nine races listed here are those not rated safe for one party or the other. The column on the right of the Table indicates whether the

Congressional Campaign Committees of the Republican and Democratic Parties have targeted each district against what they see as particularly vulnerable opposition incumbents. Most of the numbers reported here are taken from various reports of Ballotpedia, an absolutely invaluable source of data for those interested in elections.

# Appendix B: The Eighteen Most Marginal Senate Districts in 2020.

| State | Incumbent | 2014 Result | 2016 Presidential Margin | Rating |
|-------|-----------|-------------|--------------------------|--------|
| Alabama | Doug Jones (D) | Jeff Sessions 97.3* Scattering 2.7 | R +27.7 | Leans R |
| Arizona | Martha McSally (R) | See Note 1 | R +3.5 | Toss-up |
| Colorado | Cory Gardner (R) | R: Cory Gardner 48.2 D: Mark Udall* 46.3 | D +4.9 | Toss-up |
| Georgia | David Perdue | (D) R: David Perdue 52.9 D: Michelle Nunn 45.2 | R +5.2 | Likely R |
| Georgia (Special) | Johnny Isakson (R) | See Note 2 | R +5.2 | Likely R |
| Iowa | Joni Ernst (R) | R: Joni Ernst 52.1 D: Bruce Braley 43.8 | R +9.4 | Leans R |
| Kansas | Pat Roberts (R) Retiring | R: Pat Roberts* 53.1 I: Greg Orman 45.2 | R +20.6 | Likely R |
| Kentucky | Mitch McConnell | R: Mitch McConnell* 56.2 D: Alison Grimes 40.7 | R +29.8 | Likely R |
| Maine | Susan Collins (R) | R: Susan Collins* 67.0 D: Shenna Bellows 37.8 | D +3.0 | Leans R |

| | | | | |
|---|---|---|---|---|
| Michigan | Gary Peters (D) | D: Gary Peters 54.6<br>R: Terri Lynd Land 40.3 | R +2.0 | Leans D |
| Minnesota | Tina Smith (D)<br>(See Note 3) | D: Al Franken* 53.2<br>R: Mike McFadden 42.9 | D +1.5 | Likely D |
| Mississippi | Cindy Hyde-Smith (R)<br>(See Note 4) | R: Thad Cochran 59.9*<br>D: Travis Childers 37.9 | R + 17.7 | Likely R |
| Montana | Steve Daines | R: Steve Daines* 57.8<br>D: Amanda Curtis 40.1 | R +20.5 | Likely R |
| N. Hampshire | Jeanne Shaheen (D) | D: Jeanne Shaheen 51.5<br>R: Scott Brown 48.2 | D +.4 | Likely D |
| New Mexico | Tom Udall (D)<br>Retiring | D: Tom Udall* 55.6<br>R: Allen Weh 44.4 | D +8.2 | Likely D |
| North Carolina | Thom Tillis (R) | R: Thom Tillis 48.8<br>D: Kay Hagen* 47.3 | R +3.7 | Toss-up |
| Texas | John Cornyn (R) | R: John Cornyn* 61.6<br>D: David Alameel 34.4 | R +9.0 | Likely R |
| Virginia | Mark Warner (D) | D: Mark Warner* 49.1<br>R: Ed Gillespie 48.3 | D +5.3 | Likely D |

*Indicates Senators who ran as incumbents in 2014

1. This is a special election to fill the last two years of the seat held by John McCain until his death in 2018. Martha McSally (R) was appointed by the Governor to serve until a new election for a two year term is held in 2020. McSally is running.
2. This is a special election to fill the last two years of the seat held by Johnny Isakson who retired at the end of 2019. Kelly Loeffler was appointed by the Governor to serve until a new election for a two year term is held in 2020. Loeffler is running.

3. Smith (D) was appointed by the Governor to fill out the term of Al Franken who resigned in 2019. She is running for a full six year term in 2020.
4. Hyde-Smith (R) defeated Mike Espy (D) 53.6% to 46.4% in a 2018 run-off special election to replace Thad Cochran who had resigned. Hyde-Smith and Espy are expected to face off again in 2020.

Printed in the United States
By Bookmasters